Copymasters

Steve Attmore and Glyn Clarke

OXFORD

OXFORD
UNIVERSITY PRESS

Great Clarendon Street, Oxford OX2 6DP

Oxford University Press is a department of the University of Oxford.
It furthers the University's objective of excellence in research,
scholarship, and education by publishing worldwide in

Oxford   New York

Athens   Auckland   Bangkok   Bogatá   Buenos Aires   Calcutta
Cape Town   Chennai   Dar es Salaam   Delhi   Florence   Hong Kong
Istanbul   Karachi   Kuala Lumpur   Madrid   Melbourne   Mexico City
Mumbai   Nairobi   Paris   São Paolo   Singapore   Taipei   Tokyo
Toronto   Warsaw

with associated companies in Berlin and Ibadan

Oxford is a registered trade mark of Oxford University Press in the UK
and certain other countries

© Steve Attmore and Glyn Clarke 2000

The moral rights of the authors have been asserted

Database right Oxford University Press (maker)

First published 2000

All rights reserved. No part of this publication may be reproduced, stored
in a retrieval system, or transmitted, in any form or by any means, without
the prior permission in writing of Oxford University Press, or as expressly
permitted by law, or under any terms agreed with the appropriate
repropgraphics rights organization. Enquiries concerning reproduction
outside the scope of the above should be sent to the Rights Department,
Oxford University Press, at the address above.

You must not circulate this book in any other binding or cover and you
must impose this same condition on any acquirer

ISBN 0 19 913416 2

Editorial, design and production by Hart McLeod, Cambridge

Printed in Great Britain

Contents

Health, fitness and exercise	1, 2
The skeleton	3, 4
Different kinds of joints	5, 6
Muscles and movement	7, 8
Muscles and posture	9, 10
The respiratory system	11, 12
The heart	13, 14
The blood and what it does	15, 16
Circulation and exercise	17, 18
The principles of training	19, 20
Fitness	21, 22
Test your fitness	23, 24
Aerobic energy training	25, 26
Muscle training	27, 28
Effects of training	29, 30
Diet and sport	31, 32
Drugs and sport (1)	33, 34
Drugs and sport (2)	35, 36
Skill in sport	37, 38
Learning and feedback	39, 40
Motivation and goal setting	41, 42
Arousal and relaxation	43, 44
Sports injuries	45, 46
What to do in an emergency	47, 48
Leisure, recreation or sport?	49, 50
Sport for all?	51, 52
Women in sport	53, 54
Sports organizations	55, 56
Funding sport	57, 58
Sport around the world	59, 60
Sport and the media	61, 62
Other issues in sport	63, 64
Wordsearch	65, 66
Sample exam questions	67

To use this book...

Each spread deals with one major topic from the GCSE syllabus.

The left-hand pages are primarily for class work but can also be used for homework.

The right-hand pages are primarily for homework but can also be used for classwork.

Partner project pages are indicated where pupils need to work in pairs or groups.

Extension tasks are provided; these require research by the pupil and can be spread over several lessons or homeworks.

Exam-style questions (which can be used as a mock exam) are provided after worksheet 67.

The questions and exercises in this book are intended, primarily, to be used alongside the *PE to 16* classroom text book, also available from Oxford University Press.

Health, fitness and exercise

What is health?

1 Complete the following diagram. Add some more ideas.

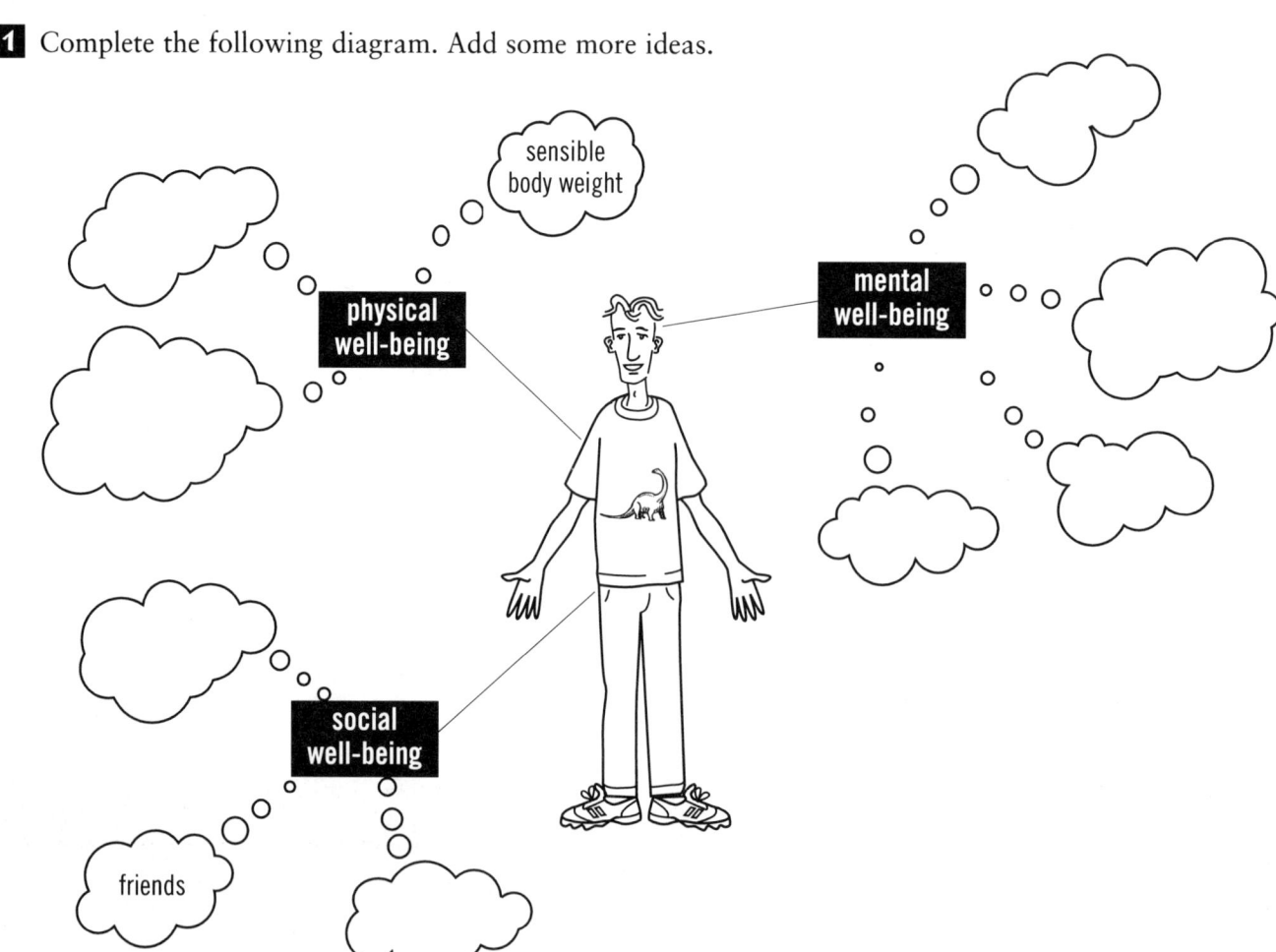

2 Skill-related fitness is a combination of the things listed in the first column below.
   a) Say why each is important.
   b) State a sport in which it is vital.

ELEMENT	WHY IT IS IMPORTANT	SPORT IN WHICH IT IS VITAL
Agility		
Balance		
Coordination		
Power		
Reaction-time		
Speed		

Health, fitness and exercise

1 Personal well-being

Match the statements below to A, B or C.

- Your self-esteem is high.
- You sulk when something upsets you.
- You've had an infection.
- You play in the school basketball team.
- Your blood pressure is normal.
- You usually do well in your homework.

A physical well-being

B mental well-being

C social well-being

2 Healthy lifestyle

A healthy lifestyle means a way of life that promotes good health.
Unscramble these anagrams to show some aspects of a healthy lifestyle.
The numbers in brackets indicate the letters in each word.
Use these words to help you: alcohol, smoking, relax, diet, sleep, exercise.

| GLUE SHEEP ON (6, 5) | SEX FOR NICER RUE (3, 3, 8) | OIL METER TAX (4, 2, 5) |
| HATE TIDY LEAH (1, 7, 4) | SNOG KIM - NO! (2, 7) | COOL LOAN, H (2, 7) |

3 Physical demands

The physical demands on the people listed below are different.
Arrange them in order, with the least demanding first.

A Traffic warden
B 70-year-old bed-ridden person
C Olympic rowing champion
D Office worker
E 16-year-old footballer
F Sumo wrestler

1st ☐   2nd ☐   3rd ☐   4th ☐   5th ☐   6th ☐

The skeleton

1 Fill in the blanks.

Your skeleton is made up of 213 _____ , held together at _____
by strong fibres called _____ .

2 Label the main bones on the skeleton.

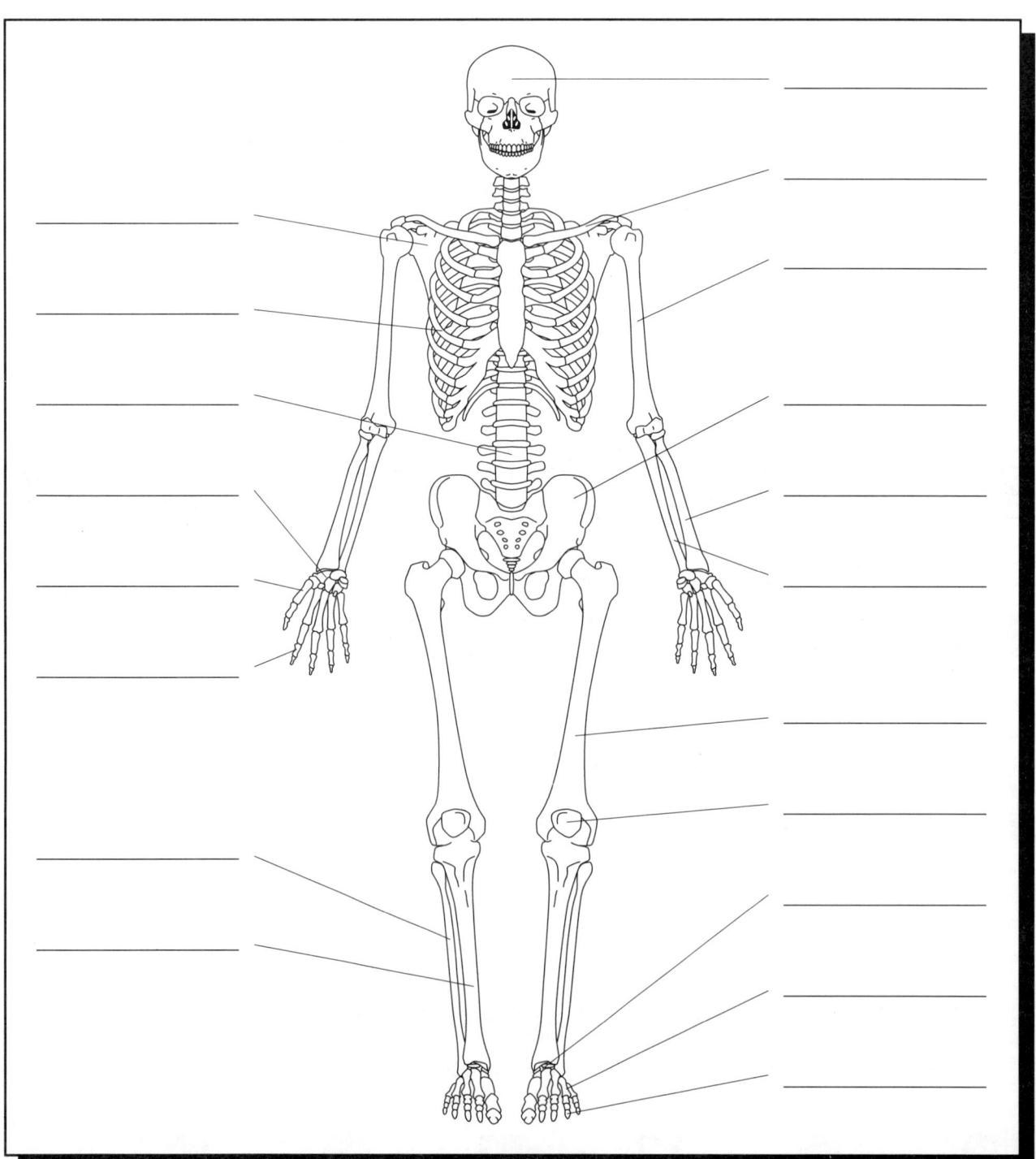

The skeleton

1 Your skeleton has four functions. What are they?

a) _____   c) _____

b) _____   d) _____

2 Give two examples of how the skeleton protects:

a) _____

b) _____

3 Give two examples of flat bones and say why they need a large surface area.

a) _____ : _____

b) _____ : _____

4 Complete this table by first writing down the scientific name of the bones listed.

Then write down the function or functions of the bone in your body.

EVERYDAY NAME	SCIENTIFIC NAME	FUNCTION(S)
Collar bone		
Backbone		
Breast bone		
Shoulder bone		
Kneecap		
Thigh bone		

Different kinds of joints

Joints are where the bones in your skeleton meet.
There are three types.

Choose the correct word(s) or *delete as necessary in the following texts.

Fixed or _____ joints.   `unmoved/immovable/removable`

The bones at an _____   `unmoved/immovable/removable`

joint can/cannot* move.
They overlap or _____   `interlink/interlock/Interlaken`
and are held together by tough
_____.   `cookies/fibre/fibroids`

Example: the joints between plates in
the _____.   `crane/cranium/geranium`

Slightly movable _____   `joists/joints/jokes`

The bones at a slightly movable
_____ can move a   `joist/joint/joke`
_____. They are held   `little/heavy load/lot`
together by straps called
_____ and joined by pads   `ligatures/signatures/ligaments`
called _____ .   `cartilage/cartridge/Carthage`

Example: joints between most
_____.   `vertebrates/vertigo/vertebrae`

Freely movable joints

At freely movable joints the bones can
move quite freely. These joints are
called _____ joints.   `sychronised/sinful/synovial`

Examples: the knee, hip
_____ and elbow joints.   `shoulder/neck/ankle`

PE to 16   Worksheet 5   © Oxford University Press

Different kinds of joints

Freely movable (synovial) joints

1 Name the five movable joints ringed on the diagram and write the name in the space provided.

2 Briefly describe the type of movement at each joint.

3 Give two examples of each movable joint.

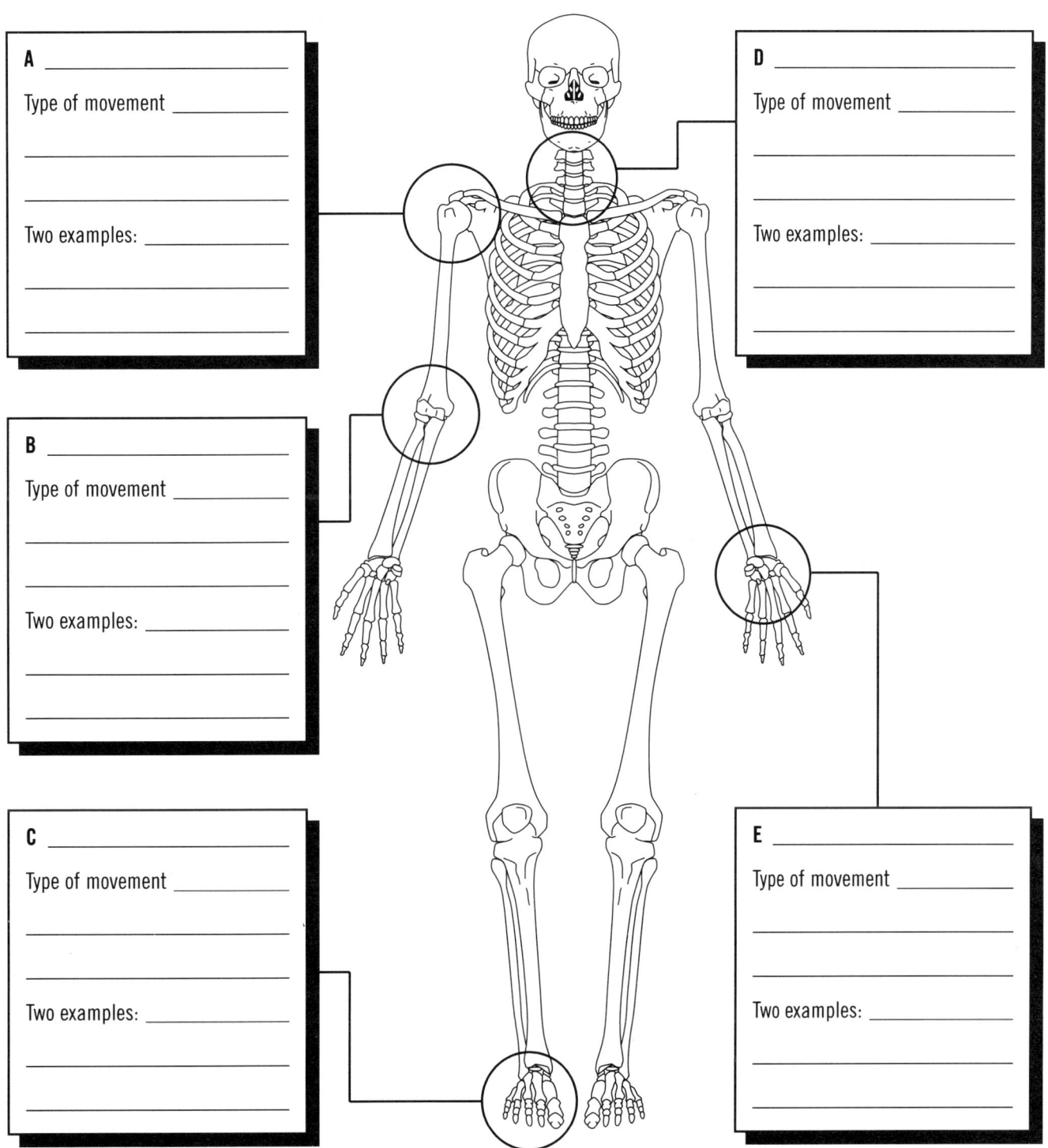

A _____

Type of movement _____

_____

_____

Two examples: _____

_____

_____

B _____

Type of movement _____

_____

_____

Two examples: _____

_____

_____

C _____

Type of movement _____

_____

_____

Two examples: _____

_____

_____

D _____

Type of movement _____

_____

_____

Two examples: _____

_____

_____

E _____

Type of movement _____

_____

_____

Two examples: _____

_____

_____

PE to 16   Worksheet 6   © Oxford University Press

Muscles and movement

1. Name the muscles of the body marked **1–11** on the diagrams below.
2. State the main action(s) of each.
3. Name a sporting activity in which the muscle is used.

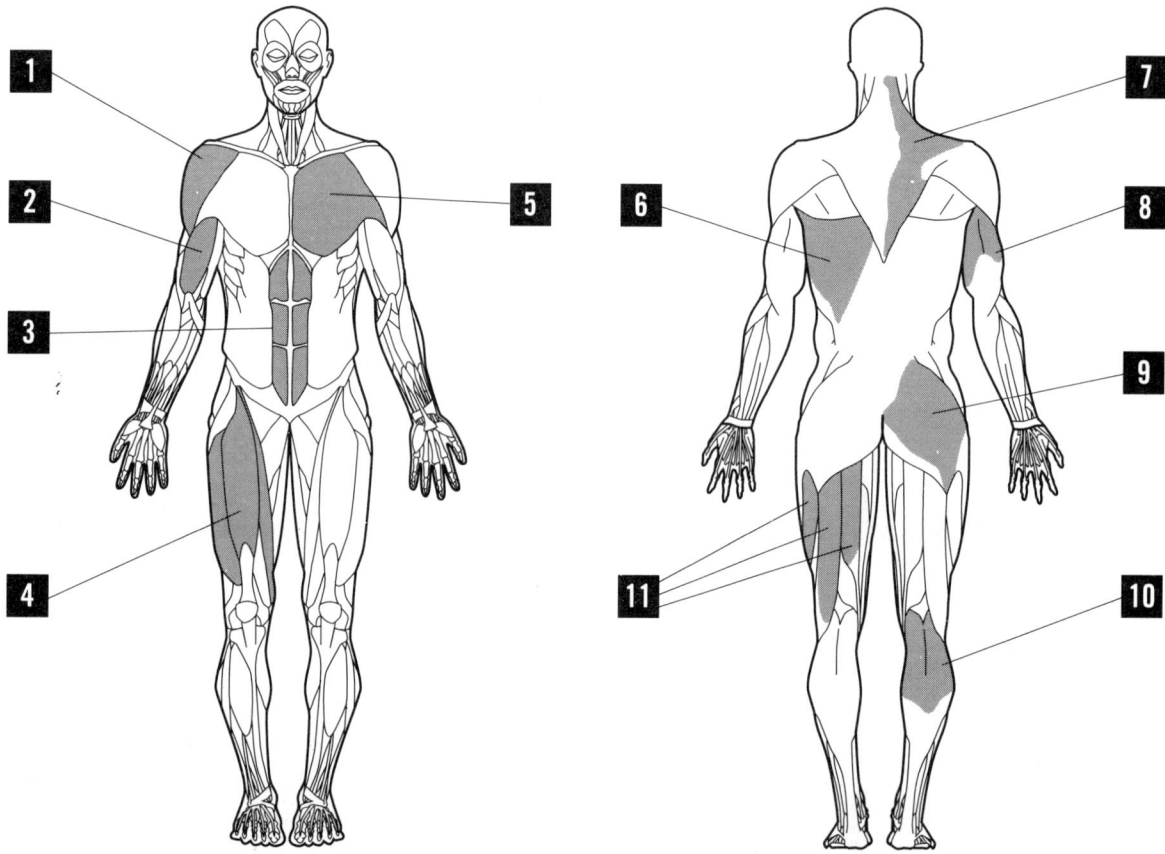

NO.	MUSCLE	MAIN ACTION(S)	SPORT
1			
2			
3			
4			
5			
6			
7			
8			
9			
10			
11			

Muscles and movement

The three kinds of muscle

1 There are three kinds of muscle at work in your body.
Give examples of each of them.

INVOLUNTARY	VOLUNTARY	CARDIAC

2 One kind of muscle works without you thinking about it.

a) What is another name for this kind of muscle? _____

b) When the muscle in artery walls contracts, what moves along the artery? _____

3 Another kind of muscle works when you want it to.

a) What is another name for this kind of muscle? _____

b) If you look at raw meat, how can you tell this type of muscle? _____

4 The third type of muscle forms the walls of your heart.

a) When this muscle contracts, it pumps _____ around the body.

b) This type of muscle is involuntary and is also called _____ muscle.

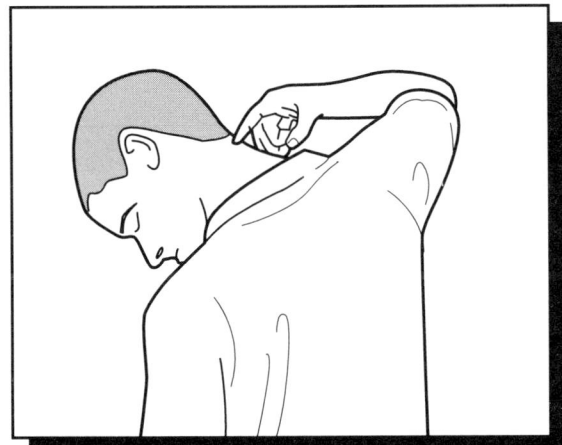

5 Put your finger on your neck like this and nod your head.

Can you feel the _____ working?

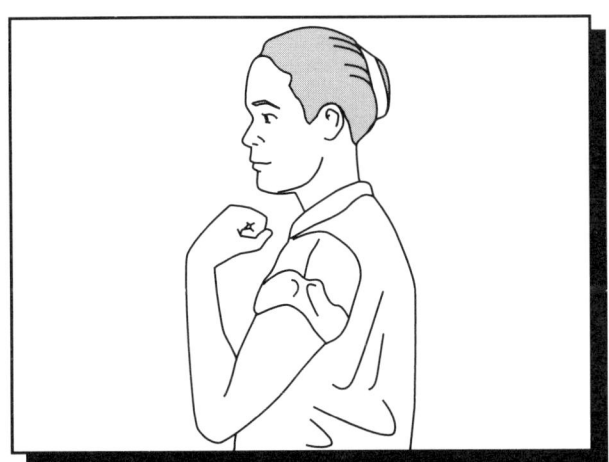

6 Let your arm hang straight, then bend it like this. A contraction of just a few centimetres in your biceps raises your fist by about 60 centimetres. What type of muscle is this an example of?

_____

Muscles and posture

1 Label the diagrams below which show muscles in the arm working in pairs.

> You will need to work with a partner.

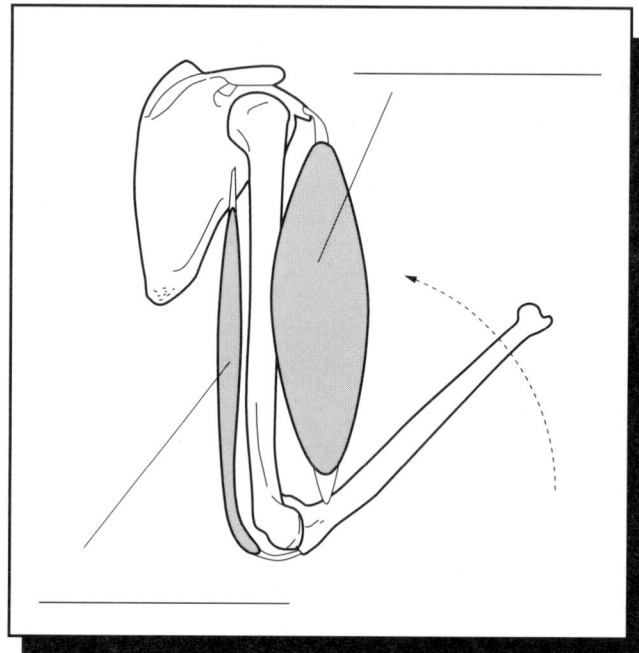 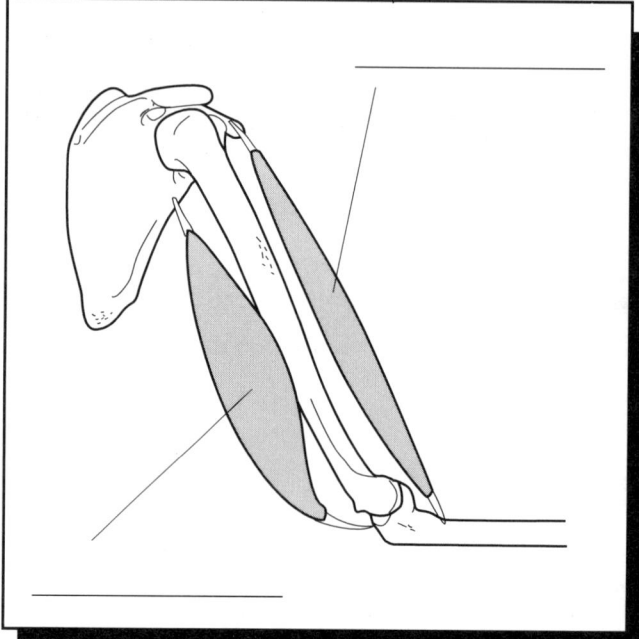

For the following questions you may need to practise the arm movements in order to answer the following questions. Work with a partner.

2 Why doesn't the humerus move when you raise your lower arm? _____

_____

3 On which bone is the origin of the biceps? _____

4 On which bone is the insertion? _____

5 On the diagrams above, mark where the insertion of the triceps is.

6 On the diagrams above, mark where the insertion of the deltoids is.

7 When a muscle contracts across a joint, usually just one bone moves. How is this helpful?

_____

_____

8 'A muscle can only have one origin.' True or false? _____

PE to 16   Worksheet 9   © Oxford University Press

Muscles and posture

The skeleton and the muscles contribute to performance in sport in different ways.

Explain the role of **(a) the skeleton, (b) muscles** in the sports and sporting activities listed.

GOALKEEPER IN SOCCER

(a) **Skeleton** – enables the goalkeeper to stand and to stop, punch or kick the ball.

(b) **Muscles** – enable the keeper to move around (leap, dive) and to punch, catch, throw or kick the ball.

HOOKER IN RUGBY FOOTBALL

BADMINTON PLAYER

FAST BOWLER IN CRICKET

GOAL SHOOTER IN NETBALL

VOLLEYBALL PLAYER

The respiratory system

1 Label each part of the respiratory system.

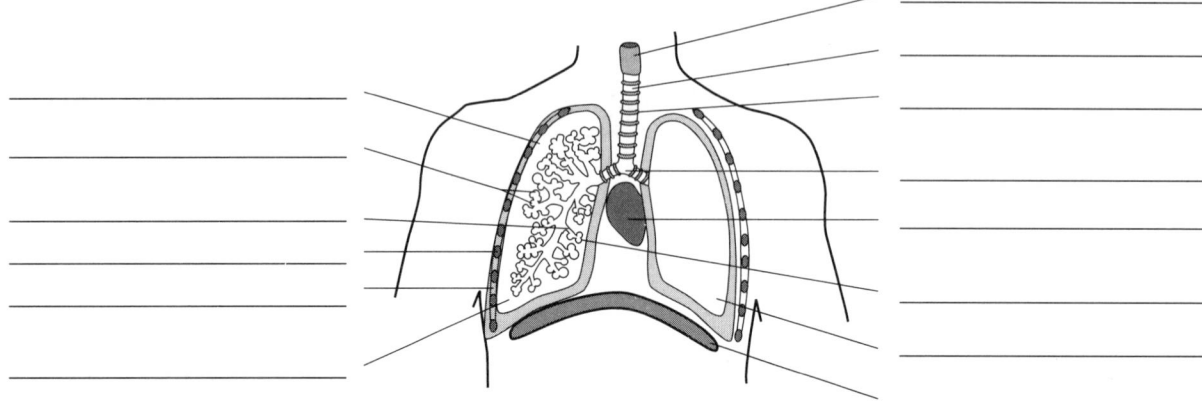

2 Complete the paragraph below, using the words from this list. You may use the word once, or not at all.

| ribs | diaphragm | volume | decrease | exhaled |
| relax | intercostal | lungs | expiration | heart |

During inspiration the _____ muscles contract and pull the _____ upwards and outwards. At the same time the _____ contracts, changing from a dome to a flatter shape. These movements cause the _____ to increase in _____. During _____ all these muscles _____, causing air to be _____.

3 Look at this table:

	% OXYGEN	% CARBON DIOXIDE
Inhaled air	21	0.03
Exhaled air during quiet breathing	17	3
Exhaled air during exercise	15	6

a) Why is there *less* oxygen in exhaled air than in inhaled air?

b) Why is there *more* carbon dioxide in exhaled air than in inhaled air?

c) Explain why the percentage of oxygen in exhaled air falls during exercise.

d) Explain why the percentage of carbon dioxide in exhaled air increases during exercise.

e) Exhaled air contains at least 15% oxygen. Explain why this makes the 'kiss of life' possible.

The respiratory system

Tidal volumes, respiratory rate and minute volumes

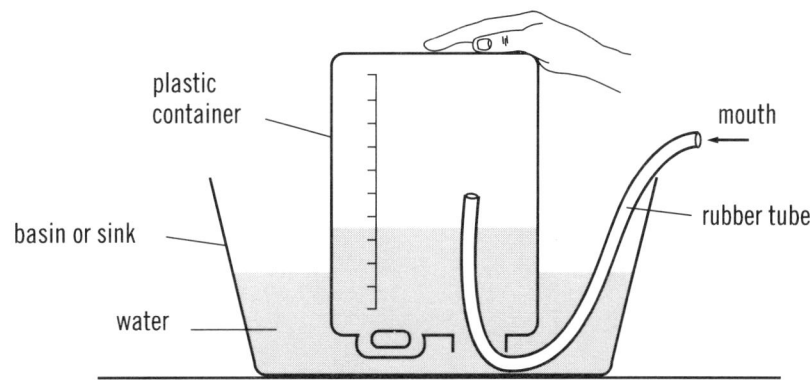

1 **Tidal volume (TV)** – the volume of air in one breath.

   a) Set up the apparatus shown above.
   b) Breathe normally into the tube. The water level will rise and fall.
   c) Ask your partner to record the maximum and minimum water levels as accurately as possible.
   d) Then work out your TV. Record the results in the table.

DURING	TV (litres)	RR (breaths per minute)	MV (litres)
Rest			
Gentle exercise			
Vigorous exercise			

2 **Respiratory rate (RR)** – the number of breaths you take per minute.

   a) Sit and relax for several minutes. Then, when your partner says, 'Go', start counting your breaths. Your partner will tell you when one minute is up. Record your results in the table.
   b) Repeat the experiment, but this time count your breaths while jogging on the spot.
   c) Repeat the experiment, but this time jog hard on the spot, raising your knees high.

3 **Minute volume (MV)** – the volume of air you breathe in per minute.

   Minute volume is given by this formula: MV = TV × RR.
   Use the formula to complete the last column in your table.

4 **Analysing the results**

   a) How have your TV, RR and MV changed with exercise?
   b) Why are these changes needed?
   c) Through training, you can increase your MV. Why would this be useful?
   d) Which muscles in particular must grow in strength for this increase to occur?
   e) Suggest an exercise you could use for this purpose.

the heart

The heart and circulation

1 In the box opposite, draw a diagram of the heart and circulation. This will serve as a useful revision exercise/exam reminder. First draw a square box for the heart in the centre of the space. Then draw a line down the middle of the box – to represent the two halves of the heart. Mark the two halves R and L for right and left. (As you are facing the drawing R is on your left!)

2 Draw two more boxes – one at the top of the space, the other at the bottom, directly above and below the 'heart'. Label the top one 'lungs' and the bottom one 'body'.

3 Draw in the blood vessels and direction of blood flow.

> R → lungs → L (Ron leaves London)
>
> L → body → R (Lessons bore Ron)

4 Label the blood vessels. Remember:
  a) **Arteries** carry blood away from the heart; **veins** carry blood to it.
  b) The main artery from the heart is the **aorta**. The main vein to it is the **vena cava**.
  c) **Pulmonary** means to do with the lungs.

5 Now draw in the four valves in the heart.
  a) 1 and 2 separate the upper and lower chambers of the heart. They are the **cuspid** valves. (1 is called the **tricuspid** valve; 2 is called the **bicuspid** or **mitral** valve.)
  b) 3 and 4 lead out of the heart. They are the **semilunar** valves.

6 The upper chambers of the heart are the atria. The lower chambers are the ventricles. Write these labels on.

The heart

How the heart pumps blood

1 Complete the following.

Use the boxed words to help you. They may be used more than once.

`valves` `close` `veins` `relax`
`atria` `blood` `arteries` `ventricles`

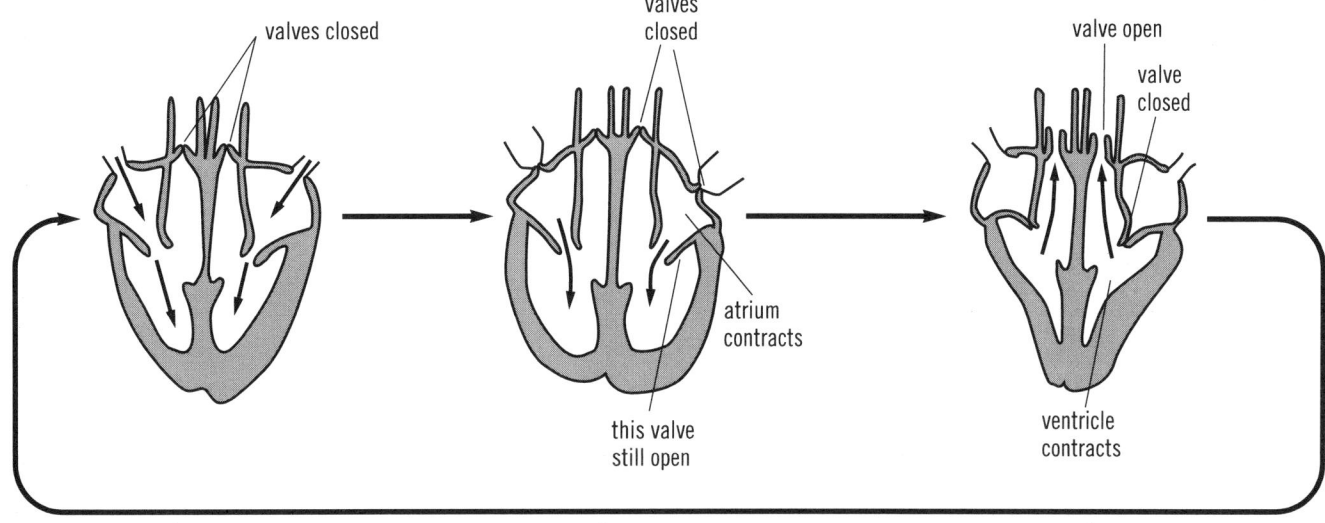

1 The heart muscle _____ .
   Both sides fill up with _____ from the _____ .

2 The _____ contract, and between the _____ the veins and the atria _____ .
   The _____ is forced into the _____ .

3 The _____ contract. The _____ between the atria and ventricles _____ .
   The blood is forced out of the _____ , into the _____ .

2 Fill in the gaps in the following sentences.

a) Steps 1–3 repeat as a cycle. It is called the _____ .

b) A heart _____ is one complete cycle.

c) The heart _____ is the number of beats per minute.

d) The _____ volume is the volume of blood pumped from the left ventricle each heart _____ .

e) The _____ output is the volume of blood pumped from the left ventricle each minute.

f) Cardiac output = _____ _____ × _____ _____ .

The blood and what it does

What's in blood?

Blood is a liquid called plasma, with red cells, white cells and platelets floating in it.
You have nearly 5 litres of it in your body – enough to fill 8 or 9 milk bottles!

Plasma

A yellow liquid (mostly water + dissolved substances).

The dissolved substances include (circle one):

a) glucose and other nutrients from digested food

b) nitrogen dioxide and other strange things

c) hormones

d) urine (hence its yellow colour)

e) carbon dioxide and other waste

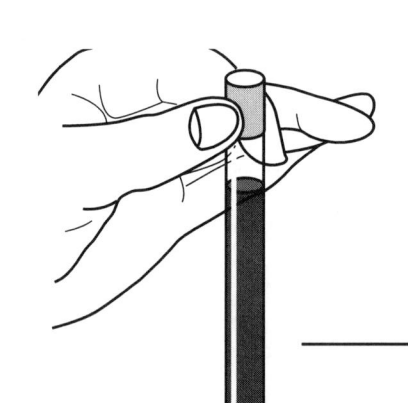

Red cells

Haemoglobin in the cells combines with oxygen.

a) What is the job of red cells?
_____
_____

b) How many red cells are found in each drop of blood?
_____
_____

c) What gives the cells their red colour?
_____
_____

White cells

There are many different types of white cell. Although they are fewer in number than red cells, you do make extra when you are ill.

a) What is the main job of white cells? _____
_____

 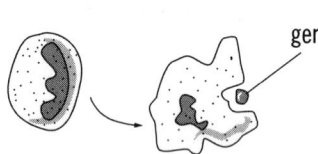

b) This type of white cell makes antibodies.

What do antibodies do?
_____
_____

c) This type squeezes through capillary walls.

Then what does it do?
_____
_____

Platelets

These are sticky fragments of cells. They stick together in cuts and make tiny fibres. Explain what happens next:

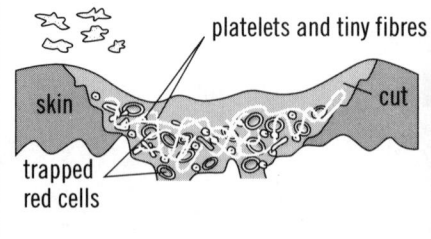

_____
_____
_____

One kind of blood cell has a nucleus. Which one? _____

NAME

The blood and what it does

Complete the paragraphs below using words from the boxed list.
You can use a word more than once, or not at all.

Your blood has two jobs: to carry things around the body and to protect you against _____.

Germs are _____ and _____ that cause _____. They enter your body through your _____, through cuts, and in food and water. _____ cause blood to _____. This stops germs getting into cuts. If germs do get into your body, some _____ _____ eat them up. Others make _____ to destroy them.

_____ makes you warm. This is because cell _____ in the muscles increases. Blood carries the _____ around your body. But when your _____ starts to rise, two things happen.

a) Blood vessels under the skin _____.

b) Heat is lost by _____.

If you get cold enough, your _____ slow down. You lose control of your _____ and you can't walk properly. You are suffering from _____.

If your body temperature drops below _____, your body tries to stop it getting colder:

a) The _____ under the skin _____.

b) Your muscles may start to _____. This produces _____.

antibodies
bacteria
blood vessels
clot
contract
disease
exercise
expand
hands
heat
hypothermia
infection
lungs
oxygen
platelets
radiation
reactions
respiration
shiver
temperature
viruses
white cells
37°C

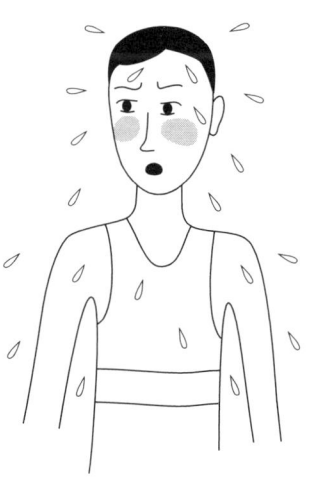

PE to 16 — Worksheet 16 — © Oxford University Press

Circulation and exercise

How to measure your heart rate

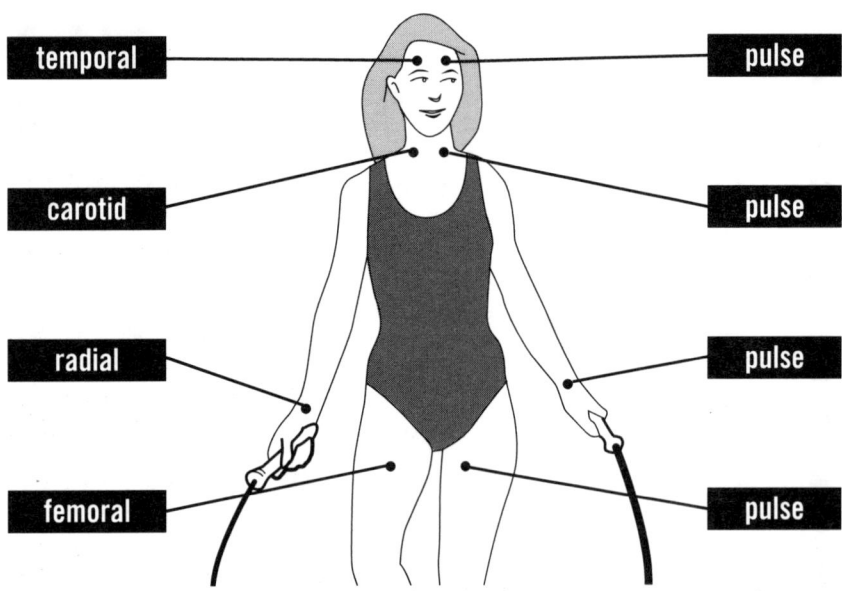

The four pulse points of the body

1 Take your pulse, using a watch with a seconds hand. Press lightly on the pulse point with your first two fingers. Note the time.
Start counting. Stop when a minute is up.   _____

2 Now do a little light exercise, such as walking up and down a flight of stairs or do sit-ups. Then take your pulse again in the same place.   _____
Has your pulse rate changed?   _____
If yes, is it higher or lower?   _____

3 Check your pulse again after 10 minutes' rest.
Has it returned to normal?   _____

4 Compare your results with a partner's.   _____

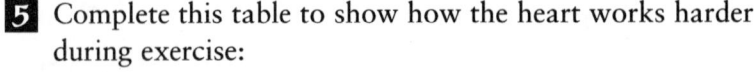

Example:
Heart rate: 68 beats a minute
Stroke volume: 75 ml per beat

Cardiac output = stroke volume x heart rate

So cardiac output = 75 x 68 ml a minute
 = 5100 ml a minute
 = 5.1 litres a minute

5 Complete this table to show how the heart works harder during exercise:

FOR A 16-YEAR-OLD	RESTING	DURING HARD EXERCISE
Heart rate (HR)	70 beats a minute	200 beats a minute
Stroke volume (SV)	70 ml per beat	150 ml per beat
Cardiac output (CO)		

PE to 16 Worksheet 17 © Oxford University Press

Circulation and exercise

Pulse rates

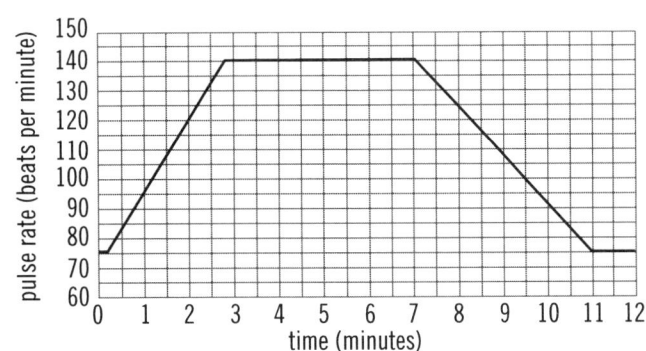

1 This graph shows how a teenager's pulse rate changed during an 8-minute run.

a) What was Kevin's resting pulse rate? _____

b) How long did it take for the pulse to reach its maximum value? _____

c) Why did Kevin's pulse rate speed up? _____

d) Did Kevin run at a steady speed, or did he try to vary it? Explain why you think so.
_____

e) After the run was over, how long did it take for Kevin's pulse to return to normal?
_____

2 a) Complete this table for the teenager in question 1. You may need to look at page 20 again to remind you of how to calculate cardiac output.

	RESTING	MAXIMUM VALUE DURING EXERCISE
Heart rate		
Stroke volume	70 ml	150 ml
Cardiac output		

b) How would you expect stroke volume and cardiac output to change during the teenager's run in question 1?

Explain why. _____
_____
_____

3 Philippa is a cyclist. Before she began competing seriously as a cyclist, her resting heart rate (HR) was 70 bpm and her resting stroke volume (SV) was 70 litres/minute.

a) Work out Philippa's resting cardiac output (CO). _____

b) Six months later Philippa's resting SV has increased to 100 litres/minute. Can you explain this change and work out her resting HR and CO?
_____
_____

PE to 16   Worksheet 18   © Oxford University Press

The principles of training

Training is a programme of exercise to help someone to get fitter. There are four basic principles in all training sessions.

Choose the correct word(s) or delete as necessary in the following texts.

1 The principle of specificity

Training must be specific for a _____ or aspect of fitness. _____ strengthens the biceps and _____ . It also increases their _____ .

This means that...
- You must/must not* decide what you want to improve.
- Then choose suitable _____ .
- Aerobic fitness, muscular endurance and similar elements of _____ are common to many _____ .

Word choices:
- sport/game/sprint
- Stretching/Chinning/Yawning
- pectorals/triceps/stomach muscles
- size/pocket money/endurance
- clothes/exercise/times
- surprise/fitness/nature
- sports/colleges/enterprises

2 The principle of _____

To make a body _____ fitter, you must overload it, or make it work harder than usual. Over _____ , the body adapts to the increased demand by getting _____ .

How to overload the body... Do it by increasing **FIT**:
- the **frequency** of exercise
- the **intensity** of exercise
- the **time** you spend exercising.

Word choices:
- overweight/overload/overboard
- part/mass/bit
- weight/here/time
- fatter/fitter/flatter

3 The principle of progression

The body can/cannot* adapt overnight to increased _____ . It can only adapt _____ . Exercising too hard, too soon, leads to _____ and other injuries.

This means that...
- You must be careful to build up your exercise level gradually, to avoid _____ .
- If you exercise at a _____ level you fitness will remain at that level.

Word choices:
- demands/stress/weight
- carefully/progressively/occasionally
- hernias/torn muscles/exhaustion
- collision/repetition/injury
- steady/ready/heady

4 The principle of reversibility

Fitness is _____ . Exercise harder and you body gets _____ . Stop exercising and it loses its _____ again.

Examples or reversibility
- Strength training makes your muscles thicken. This is called _____ .
- When you stop training they will _____ again.
- Muscles that are not used will waste away or _____ .

Word choices:
- painful/reversible/fanatical
- thinner/fitter/fatter
- shape/fitness/energy
- hypothermia/hypertrophy/hypnosis
- multiply/disappear/shrink
- atrophy/two trophies/autotroph

PE to 16 — Worksheet 19 — © Oxford University Press

NAME

The principles of training

Plan a 6-week fitness training programme

1 Plan a fitness training programme for someone you know.
Find out about the person it's for. Ask questions:

- How old?
- Reasons for wanting to get fitter?
- Any injuries?
- Play a sport?
- Living near a sports facility?
- How fit right now?
- Any health problems?
- Any likes and dislikes in exercise?
- Sociable?

2 Decide what aspects of fitness need improving.
This depends on what the person wants to get fitter for.

3 Plan the **FIT** programme.

Frequency: How often should the person exercise?
Intensity: How hard should the person exercise?
Time: How long should each session last?

What exercises or other activities will help this person to achieve the fitness goals?

4 Now complete this chart for the chosen person's 6-week fitness training programme.

Week	1	2	3	4	5	6
Frequency						
Time						
Distance/number						

NAME

Fitness

Activities to try

1 Try activities A–D below with a partner. When one of you has tried an activity, swap over and let your partner have a go. For each activity record your score, and that of your partner.

A Stand on one foot with your eyes closed. Time how long you can balance. Record the best score of two attempts.

B Hold your arm straight in front of you. Count how many times you can tightly clench and unclench your fist in 30 seconds. Only one attempt allowed.

C Stand 1 metre behind your partner and throw a tennis ball over your partner's shoulder without warning. How many times out of ten attempts does your partner catch the ball before it bounces twice?

D Mark out an area 5 m long and 1 m wide. Place four cones as shown. Time how long it takes to run in and out between all the cones. Record the best time of two attempts.

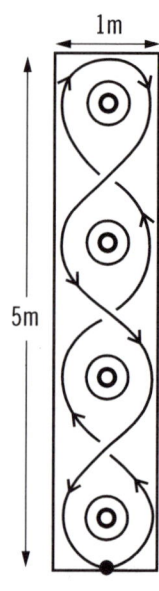

2 In your group, compare your best scores for the four activities.

a) Why are there differences in scores between individuals of a similar age?
_____

b) Which aspect of fitness is being tested. (There may be more than one.)
_____

c) Name two sports where this aspect of fitness is very important.
_____

d) Give two examples of how this aspect of fitness is needed in everyday life.
_____

NAME

Fitness

Somatotyping

Somatotyping looks at how fat **(A)**, how muscular **(B)** and how linear **(C)** you are, in that order. Each is measured on a scale of **1** to **7**. Most people have a rating such as **3 4 4**, **3 5 2** or **4 3 3**.

A Extreme **endomorph**
Somatotype rating: **7 1 1**

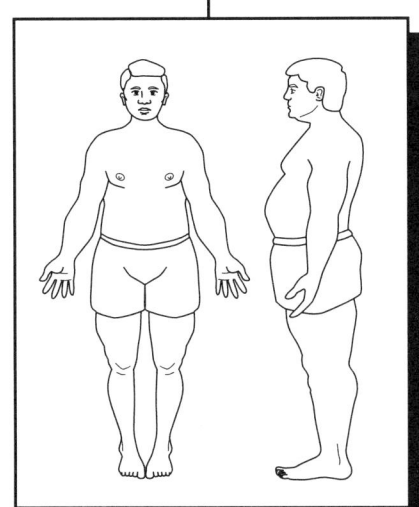

B Extreme **mesomorph**
Somatotype rating: **1 7 1**

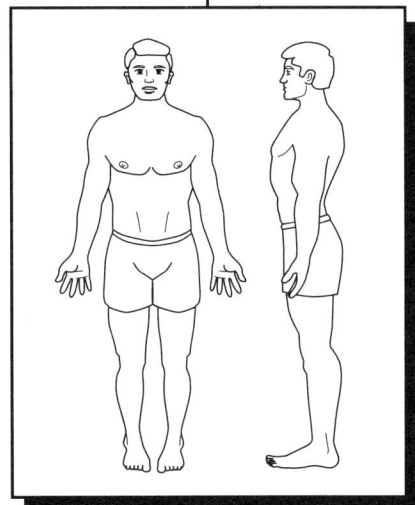

C Extreme **ectomorph**
Somatotype rating: **1 1 7**

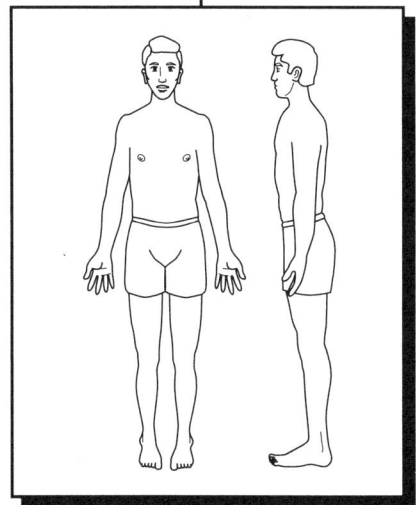

1 Match these descriptions to **A**, **B** or **C**:

a) Broad muscular shoulders and narrow hips ☐

b) Thin, narrow chest and shoulders ☐

c) Plump and pear-shaped ☐

2 a) Have a guess at your own somatotype rating.
Mark it on the diagram.

b) Give ratings to other members of your family, or friends.
Add them to the diagram.

3 Match the somatotype ratings to the most suitable sport.

a) **6 5 2** ☐   **i) volleyball**

b) **2 4 3** ☐   **ii) wrestling**

c) **4 6 3** ☐   **iii) cycling**

d) **2 5 4** ☐   **iv) American football**

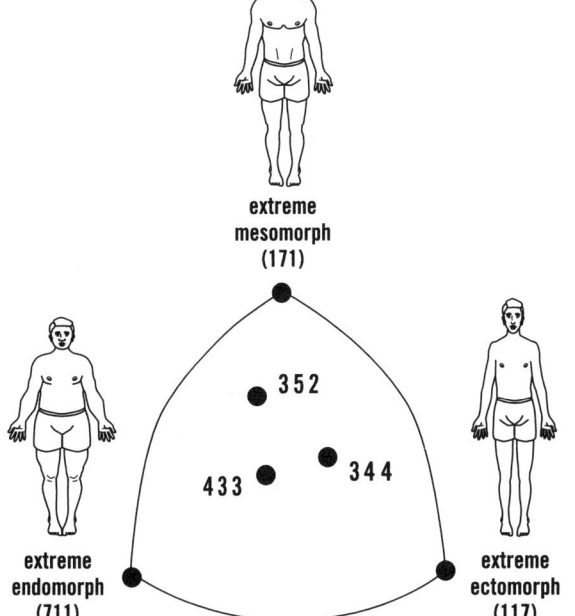

Somatotypes can be shown on a somatochart like this one.

PE to 16   Worksheet 22   © Oxford University Press

NAME

Test your fitness

These exercises will test your general level of fitness.

You will need:
a partner to work with; a stop watch or a watch with a seconds hand; a 50-metre space; a measure for marking out the running track; a bar to pull yourself up (for the chins test).

1 30-metre sprint

1. Measure out a 30-metre track. Mark the start and finish lines.
2. Stand about 20 metres behind the start line.
3. When your partner shouts 'Go', sprint as fast as you can to the finish line.
4. Your partner should record your speed in seconds, from the moment you cross the start line.

2 The sit-up test

1. Lie on the floor with your hands touching your head behind your ears, knees bent at 90°, and feet flat on the floor.
2. Get your partner to hold your feet down.
3. Raise your trunk until your elbows are past your knees, then lower yourself again. This is one sit-up.
4. Do as many as you can in 30 seconds. Record your result.

3 The chins test

1. Hang from the bar with your palms facing inwards.
2. Raise yourself until your chin is level with the bar, then lower yourself until your arms are straight again.
3. Repeat until you are too tired to do anymore. Record how many you did in the grid.

Now swap over roles and let your partner try the tests.

Fitness scores

YOU		
Test	Date	Score
Sprint		
Sit-ups		
Chins		

YOUR PARTNER		
Test	Date	Score
Sprint		
Sit-ups		
Chins		

Try the tests a week or so later to see if your performance improves.

NAME

Test your fitness

The most important factor in fitness is the ability of your heart and lungs to deliver oxygen, and your muscles to use it. Try these tests on your own.

You will need:
a stool or low bench (about 50 cm high); a stop watch or timer; two tennis balls; a high wall (such as the side of a house); some talcum powder or chalk; a tape measure.

1 Harvard step test

1. Step on the bench or stool at a rate of 30 steps a minute for 5 minutes. If you can't keep up, stop after 20 seconds of slower steps.
2. Rest for 1 minute, then take your pulse for 15 seconds.
3. Your aerobic fitness is worked out using this formula:

$$\text{Score} = \frac{\text{length of exercise in seconds} \times 100}{5.5 \times \text{pulse count}}$$

The higher it is, the fitter you are. Can you see why?
_____

2 The vertical jump test

1. Cover the palm of your hand in talcum powder or chalk dust.
2. Stand sideways to the wall with your feet flat on the ground.
3. Flex your knees and jump as high as you can, making a mark on the wall as high up as possible.
4. Repeat three times. Work out how high you jumped each time.
_____

Now try this test for hand-eye co-ordination.

3 A test for co-ordination

1. Hold a tennis ball in each hand. Start bouncing both balls at the same time.
2. Count how many times you can bounce both together without making a mistake.
3. Record the best score of two attempts. _____

Aerobic energy training

1 Continuous training

You walk, jog or cycle at a steady pace, without a rest. Build up the time slowly, especially if you are unfit (see pages 24–25 for fitness tests).

2 Fartlek training

You can use this method for running, cycling and skiing.

Example: here is part of a 30-minute Fartlek running session.

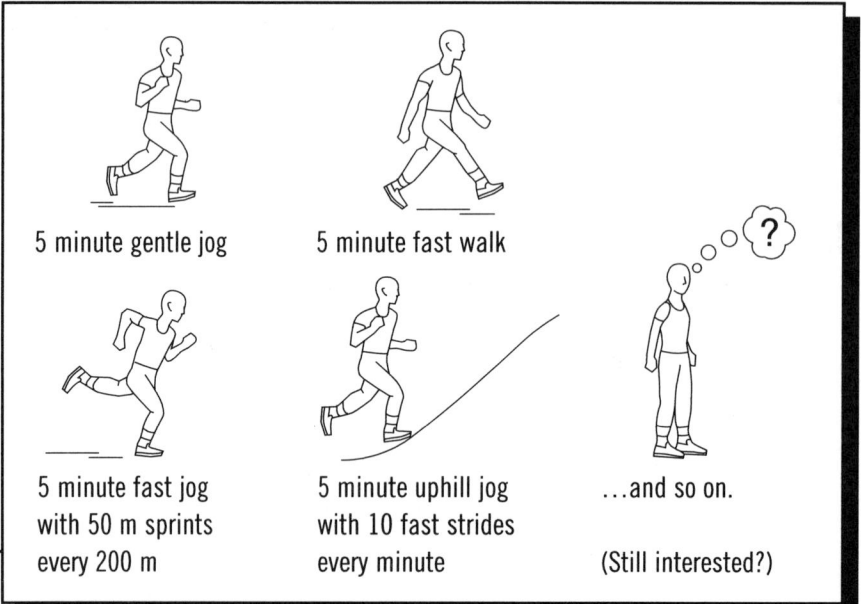

5 minute gentle jog

5 minute fast walk

5 minute fast jog with 50 m sprints every 200 m

5 minute uphill jog with 10 fast strides every minute

…and so on.
(Still interested?)

3 Interval training

This method has a fixed pattern of fast and slow work. You can use it for things like running and swimming. Each repetition of the pattern is called a rep. You must complete a set of reps before you can rest.

Example:

30 seconds sprint   then…   30 seconds easy jogging

4 Aerobics

You exercise every part of the body in time to music. To avoid damaging your joints, work on a sprung hardwood floor or soft mat; or else choose low impact aerobics.

Complete this grid

	NAME ONE ADVANTAGE	NAME ONE DISADVANTAGE	SAY WHAT KIND(S) OF FITNESS IT WILL IMPROVE
Continuous training			
Fartlek training			
Interval training			
Aerobics			

Aerobic energy training

For each of the activities below:

a) what kind of fitness is being improved

b) name two effects it will have on your body

c) name two sports where it will help you.

Muscle training

> Muscular strength is the amount of force that you can produce when you contract your muscles.

1 With a partner, make a list of 12 sports that need a high degree of muscular strength.

1 _____	5 _____	9 _____
2 _____	6 _____	10 _____
3 _____	7 _____	11 _____
4 _____	8 _____	12 _____

2 Select one of the sports you chose in 1 and explain the need for muscular strength.

Name of sport: _____

Need for muscular strength: _____

_____

_____

3 This graph shows how a healthy 15-year-old's heart rate changed during a training run.

Discuss the following questions with your partner. Write down your answers in note form.

a) Is she fit or unfit? Explain why you think so. _____

b) What do you think she was doing between A and B? _____

c) Between what points was she jogging at an easy pace? _____

d) At what point did she speed up in her run? _____

e) Would you say she was working anaerobically at any point? Explain your answer.

_____

Muscle training

Improving muscular strength and endurance

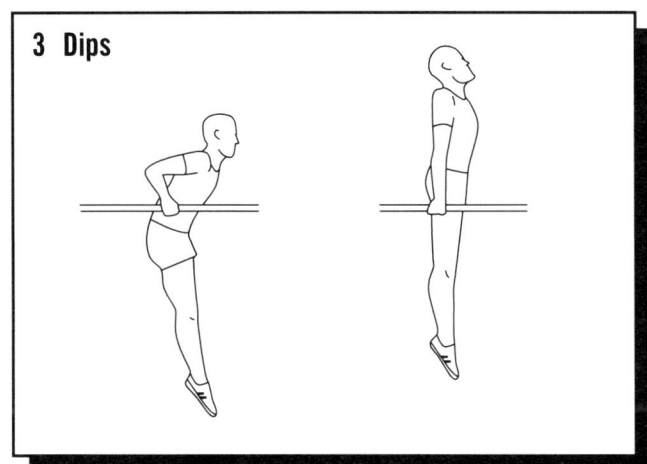
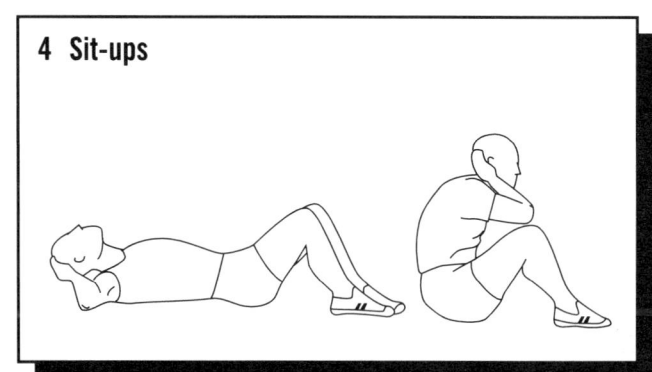

1 Complete the following sentences.

♦ Tests 1–3 above test your strength and/or endurance of _____ and _____ muscles.

♦ If the test lasts longer than 30–60 seconds, it is testing _____ rather than strength.

♦ Test 4 tests the strength and/or endurance of the _____ muscles.

2 Think of other muscle groups. Name other tests to improve endurance of these muscle groups.

One example has been provided for you.

	MUSCLE GROUP	TEST
1	legs	squat thrusts
2		
3		
4		
5		
6		
7		

Effects of training

Estimating your heart rate

You can get a good idea of your heart rate from how hard you feel you are working.

This table shows feelings on a scale from 6 to 20.
You find your estimated heart rate by multiplying the rating by 10.
For example, if an exercise feels very very light its rating is 7.
Your estimated heart rate is therefore 7 x 10 = 70.

HOW THE EXERCISE FEELS	RATING
Very very light	6
	7
	8
Very light	9
	10
Fairly light	11
	12
Somewhat hard	13
	14
Hard	15
	16
Very hard	17
	18
Very very hard	19
	20

Try the following in a group of three or four. Compare your results. It is not a competition!

1 Do 3 minutes of what you feel is very very light activity (rating 7). For example, it could be gently swinging your arms.

Now measure your pulse for 10 seconds.
What is your heart rate in beats per minute? _____

How close is it to 70? _____

2 Now do 3 minutes of what feels like hard activity (rating 15). For example, it could be running hard on the spot, raising your knees as high as you can.

Take your pulse immediately for 10 seconds.
What is your heart rate in beats per minute? _____

How close is it to 150? _____

3 Repeat for different activities until your feelings match the heart rate scale. How do your feelings compare with those of others in the group?

_____
_____
_____
_____

An isometric exercise

Sit against a wall in the position shown.
Time how long you can stay this way.
The pain shows that lactic acid has built up. So your leg muscles are working even though you are still.

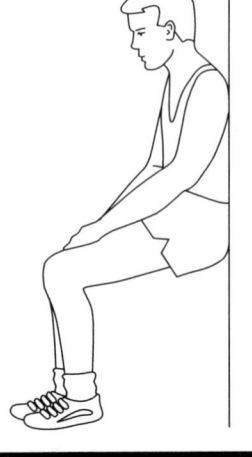

PE to 16   Worksheet 29   © Oxford University Press

Effects of training

Complete the passage below about the effects of training.
Every time you come across a missing word choose one from
the three possible answers in the boxes.

Months of training can make big changes in your _____. Over months of swimming, jogging or _____ your _____ grows bigger. It holds more blood and contracts more strongly. Your heart becomes a more efficient _____.

(body/wallet/metabolism)
(knitting/cycling/yodelling)
(thighs/muscle/heart)
(organ/pump/vein)

Aerobic training also increases the efficiency of your _____ and respiratory system. This means that you can move _____ to the muscles faster and get rid of carbon dioxide faster. So you don't get _____ so fast.

(lungs/stomach/knee)
(oxygen/mountains/anything)
(a spare tyre/winded/tired)

You need to train at least _____ times a week, otherwise it will not be effective. If you overtrain, you may experience _____ and joint pains, problems in sleeping, and loss of _____. You may find yourself feeling _____ and tired and get more than your normal share of colds and _____.

(three/thirteen/thirty)
(hallucinations/soreness/numbness)
(earnings/hair/appetite)
(anxious/queasy/depressed)
(hots/flus/fevers)

Anaerobic exercise puts a lot of stress on your heart and _____. This means it can be dangerous. If you are _____, you should do several weeks of aerobic training before you start on _____.

(nervous system/circulatory system/heating system)
(lousy/unfit/nosey)
(anaerobic training/a diet/acrobatics)

For anaerobic training you use all-out effort during the activity. After each all-out effort, take a _____ so that your body has time to pay off the oxygen debt and remove _____ _____.

(rest/snack/anything)
(carbon dioxide/the furniture/lactic acid)

PE to 16 — Worksheet 30 — © Oxford University Press

Diet and sport

1 Match each substance **A–E** to one of the statements **(i)–(v)**.

A water
B carbohydrates
C iodine
D fibre
E iron

(i) helps move food through your gut faster
(ii) your blood could not carry oxygen without it
(iii) the body's first choice for energy
(iv) is found in every cell in the body
(v) needed for the hormones that control how fast you burn up food

2 Below is a list of people each having a different lifestyle and therefore a different energy need. The amount of food each person has to eat, to match needs, is therefore different.

Arrange these in order of how much they need to eat.
The person who needs to eat the least should come first.

- a male student of 17
- a retired woman of 75
- a landscape gardener of 40
- a boy of 12
- a female student of 17

1 _____
2 _____
3 _____
4 _____
5 _____

3 1 kg of body fat is equivalent to 32,000 kJ of energy. Suppose your energy needs are 10,000 kJ per day, and you eat enough food to provide 14,000 kJ per day.

a) How much more energy do you take in per day than you need?

b) Are you eating too much food for your needs, or too little?

c) What happens to this extra food?

d) At this rate, how long would it take you to gain an extra kilogram in weight?

Diet and sport

For the following you will need to:
- weigh yourself
- use a calculator
- obtain the label from at least one chocolate bar
- get hold of one packet of crisps

1 This table shows the amount of energy burned up per kilogram of body weight per minute, for different levels of activity.

ENERGY USED IN	KJ PER KILOGRAM PER MINUTE
Resting	0.13
Moderate exercise (eg jogging or swimming)	0.59
Vigorous exercise (eg football or netball)	0.79

a) Calculate how much energy you burn up per minute when you are resting.
   `0.13 kJ x your weight`

b) Calculate how much you burn up per minute during moderate exercise.
   `0.59 kJ x your weight`

c) Calculate how much you burn up per minute during vigorous exercise.
   `0.79 kJ x your weight`

2 If you weigh 60 kg, a chocolate bar provides 960 kJ of energy and you burn up 7.8 kJ of energy per minute when resting, how long will it take you to burn up the energy from the chocolate bar?
   `Clue: 960 ÷ 7.8 minutes`

a) Look at your chocolate bar labels. How much energy do the bars provide?

b) Work out how many minutes it would take you to use up this energy during vigorous exercise.

c) Look at the crisps packet. How much energy do the crisps provide?

d) Work out how long it would take to work off this energy during moderate exercise.

Keep a record of everything you eat for one week.

a) Try to work out what proportion of carbohydrates, fats and proteins you ate. (Labels on food packets will help you.)

b) Estimate how much energy this food has provided. Then work out your average daily energy intake.

c) Assume your energy needs are 11,000 kJ if you are male and 9,000 kJ if you are female. Did you eat too much? Or too little?

d) Did you eat a healthy balanced diet? Explain.

NAME

Drugs and sport (1)

A drug is any chemical substance you take that affects the way your body works. Most drugs are developed for medical purposes. They are dangerous when misused.

Doping means taking drugs to improve sporting performance. It is a big problem in sport.

1 In a group, spend 10 minutes discussing the following.

   a) What do the above images have in common?

   b) What effect can each have on your performance in sport?

2 Now spend 5 minutes brainstorming a list of reasons why athletes take drugs. Brainstorming means writing ideas on a large sheet of paper or a whiteboard without stopping to discuss whether they are good ideas or not.

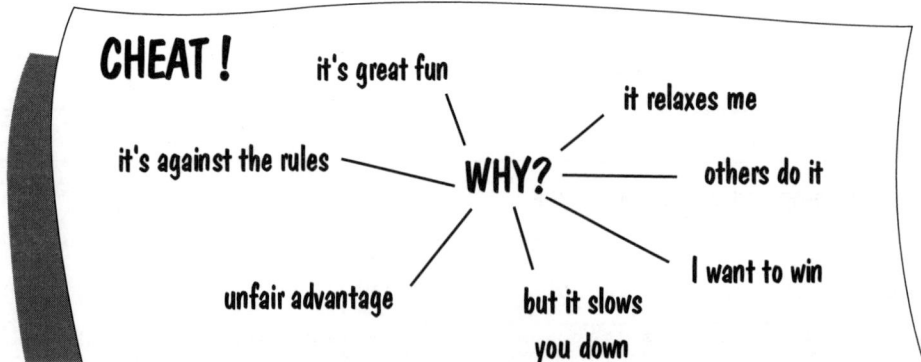

3 Look at the brainstormed ideas and try to write a list of 'pros' and 'cons' for taking drugs to aid your sporting performance. Are any of the reasons for taking drugs of any sort justifiable?

NAME

Drugs and sport (1)

You have been asked to prepare an article for the school magazine on the use of drugs in sport today. First, you need to find out useful information to back up your arguments. The suggestions below may help in your preparation.

A Why should sports people **not** use drugs? Write down as many reasons as you can.

Which reason do *you* think is the most important?

B Can you think of any reasons why sports people should be allowed to take banned drugs? Write them down.

C Write down two harmful effects of using:

   a) stimulants _____ _____

   b) anabolic steroids _____ _____

   c) painkillers during exercise. _____ _____

D Which substance in alcohol makes you drunk? _____

Write down five ways in which alcohol will affect a competitor's performance during a sports event.

E Cigarettes contain an addictive substance, which is poisonous. What is it? _____

Cigarette packets carry a message. What is it? _____

Name five ways in which smoking is harmful.

F Find out more information from the library or the internet.

These websites may be useful: www.hedweb.com   www.magic.mb.ca   www.resource-net.isdd.co.uk

Make a note of any other useful websites you find.

You should now be ready to write your article. Turn to worksheet 36.

Drugs and sport (2)

Following on from your brainstorming and discussion session (page 34), complete the chart below. Some have been provided for you.

Think of as many examples of drugs, their effects and associated sports as you can.

You can use any notes you have to help you.

DRUG TYPE	EXAMPLES	EFFECTS	ASSOCIATED SPORTS
Stimulant	Amphetamine Caffeine	◆ ◆ ◆ ◆ ◆ ◆	Cycling
◆	Beta blockers Benodiazepine	◆ ◆ ◆ ◆ ◆ ◆	Snooker
Narcotic analgesics (painkillers)	◆ ◆ ◆	Drowsiness ◆ ◆	Cycling
Anabolic agents	◆	◆ ◆ ◆	Contact sports
Diuretics		Get rid of fluid from the body Help reduce body weight ◆ ◆	

NAME

Drugs and sport (2)

Having done your research (page 34), you should now start writing your magazine article. Don't put it off any longer!

Remember that a good article includes:
- an eye-catching headline
- an attention-grabbing opening paragraph
- information to back up the views stated
- a cross-section of opinion
- a conclusion that states your point of view.

1 Write a first draft of the article.

Remember to include pictures and/or graphs.

Use the space below to make a note of where to obtain any useful pictures and/or graphs.

Where to find pictures / graphs

2 Read through your first draft.

Have you made your points sensibly and clearly?

Have you included all the things suggested in the box above?

Remember who you are writing for: your peers, younger students and possibly parents.

3 Edit your article to make sure there are no mistakes.

Check the spelling, grammar and punctuation.

4 Prepare the final copy. Make the presentation neat – and don't forget to add your name.

Skill in sport

> Skill is the learned ability to bring about a pre-determined result with maximum certainty and maximum efficiency.

What does this mean?

1 a) Time yourself against a partner. In two minutes, see how many team skills you can name (eg passing in football).

Write them down. _____
_____
_____
_____

b) Do the same with skills that you might perform on your own (eg throwing the discus).

Write them down. _____
_____
_____
_____

2 Do the same as for 1, but for one particular team sport and one particular individual activity.

3 For this activity you will need: two tennis rackets and two tennis balls.

a) Count how many times you can bounce a ball on the racket without dropping it.
_____

b) Now use the racket to bounce the ball on the ground. Count how many times you can do it without missing it. _____

c) Try a and b together, with one racket in each hand. Count how many times you can do both together.
_____

d) In which step did your brain have most information to deal with: a, b or c?
_____

PE to 16   Worksheet 37   © Oxford University Press

Skill in sport

If a skill is affected a lot by what is going on around the player or performer, then it is said to be more **open**. If a skill is not affected much by what is going on around, then it is said to be more **closed**. Most sports fall somewhere between closed and open.

1 Look at the diagram below. This is called a **continuum**. It runs from 'open' to 'closed'.

Mark these sports on the continuum:

- Swimming
- Rugby football
- Archery
- Badminton
- Gymnastics
- Potholing

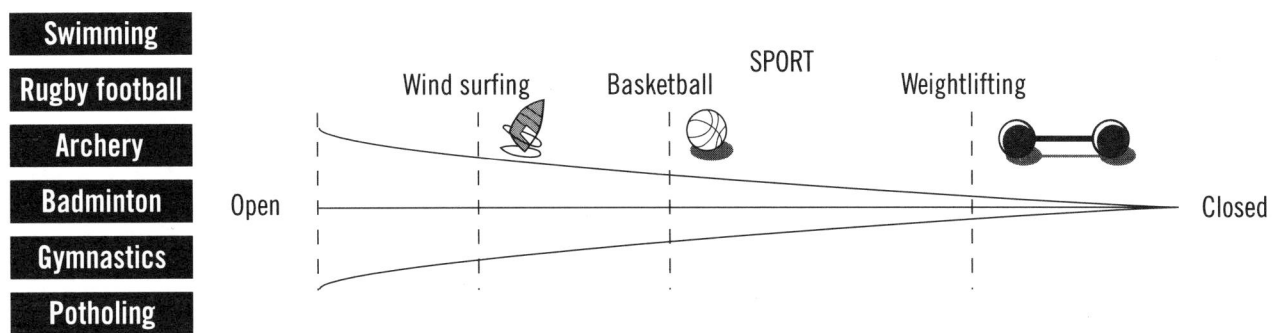

2 Mark these sports skills on the continuum below which runs from 'easy' to 'difficult':

- A free throw in basketball
- The front crawl in swimming
- Taking a penalty in football
- Putting in golf
- Tacking in windsurfing
- Dribbling in hockey

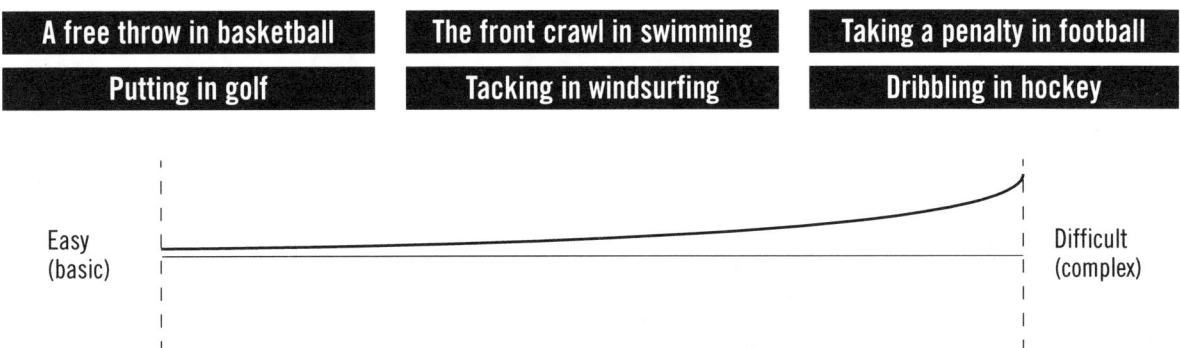

Investigating proprioception (the sense of muscular position)

Stand with your arms stretched out straight and level in front of you. Close your eyes. Swing one arm up and the other down. Now return your arms to their original position.

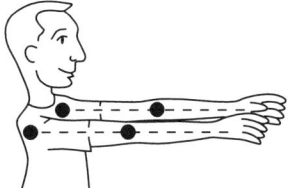 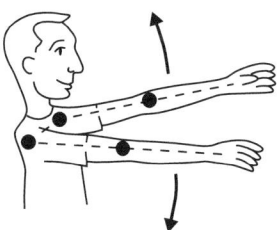

When you think they're back where they started, open your eyes and check.

With your eyes closed, you depend on proprioception to know the position of your arms. If they were level when you checked, it shows good proprioception.

Learning and feedback

If you want to learn fast and well, pay attention to feedback! Feedback is the response you get to your performance. For example when learning a new skill your score might rise the more you practise it, or your opponent might miss the shot, or your trainer might say 'Well done'.

Divide your group into three. You need at least two people in each group. Those in Group A can work alone. Those in B and C will work in pairs. Each group has the same task: *to draw ten 5-cm lines while blindfolded.*

a) Group A will receive no feedback, group B will receive knowledge of results (KR) only, and group C will receive knowledge of performance (KP).

b) One person in each pair measures the lines and provides feedback.

c) When you measure a line write the measurement beside it, to help you compare the results.

GROUP A	GROUP B	GROUP C
Put on the blindfold and draw the ten lines. Now measure them to see how you did.	After each attempt, the person providing feedback measures the line and calls out 'Yes' or 'No'. He or she says nothing more.	After each attempt, the person providing feedback describes how close the attempt was to success, and gives some encouragement. For example 'Good. Just half a centimetre too short.'

Compare the results for the three groups.

Which group gave the best performance? _____

What does that teach you about feedback? _____

_____

_____

_____

NAME

Learning and feedback

Learning a new skill is a complex process. There are three recognised phases in skill learning:

◆ **Cognitive** – the first stage in learning a skill is to understand what needs to be done. Beginners need to be shown or told what actions they have to do and what results from these actions.

◆ **Associative** – with practice, performance of the skill improves considerably.

◆ **Autonomous** – by this phase, the skills are performed almost automatically without much thought to what is being done.

If we use tennis as an example, this is how the three phases apply to learning a new skill:

Cognitive phase: to perform a tennis serve, the ball needs to be hit over the net to start the game.

Associative phase: to perform a tennis serve well, the ball should be hit low over the net and into the opposite service box.

Autonomous phase: during a tennis serve, the ball can be hit low over the net to the opposing player's backhand or forehand depending on where the player is standing. The aim is to prevent your opponent returning the serve.

Working with a partner, select a sport or game you like (excluding tennis). Try to teach your partner a skill. Split the skill into the three phases. What should be happening at each phase? (Your partner may not reach the autonomous phase as this is a highly developed stage only reached after lots of practice.)

Sport / game	

PHASE	WHAT YOU TAUGHT THE OTHER PERSON TO DO	HOW DID THE TEACHING GO? BE HONEST
Cognitive		
Associative		
Autonomous		

PE to 16 — Worksheet 40 — © Oxford University Press

NAME

Motivation and goal setting

Investigating motivation

You will need:
- a start line marked on the floor
- a tape measure
- prizes for the best performers (say Mars bars).

a) Randomly choose three groups A, B and C, with 4 people in each group. Each person will do 3 standing broad jumps. All jumps are recorded, not just the longest.

b) Group A goes first. This group does the jumps in private, away from the class, and gets no feedback *of any kind*.

c) Group B goes next. This group works in private. But before starting, the group is told that the two best performers will get a prize. Say what the prize is.

d) Group C goes last. This group jumps in front of the class. There is no prize, but the class is very encouraging and gives friendly and positive feedback. For example, the class can cheer.

e) The average longest jump for each group is calculated, by adding the 4 longest jumps and dividing by 4.

f) Compare the results of the three groups. What do you notice? Explain it using the idea of motivation. Which kind of motivation worked best?

GROUP A	1ST JUMP	2ND JUMP	3RD JUMP	LONGEST
Jumper 1				
Jumper 2				
Jumper 3				
Jumper 4				

GROUP B	1ST JUMP	2ND JUMP	3RD JUMP	LONGEST
Jumper 1				
Jumper 2				
Jumper 3				
Jumper 4				

GROUP C	1ST JUMP	2ND JUMP	3RD JUMP	LONGEST
Jumper 1				
Jumper 2				
Jumper 3				
Jumper 4				

Motivation and goal setting

1 Think of a sport that you are involved in. Write down in the space below some reasons why you like taking part in that sport. Then write next to the reasons **extrinsic** or **intrinsic** depending on whether you feel that the drive to do this sport comes from outside or inside yourself.

2 Copy and complete each statement using one term from the boxed list. You must use the term once only:

| an object | direct aggression |
| indirect aggression | aggressive attitude |

a) A rugby tackle is an example of _____.

b) An overhead smash in tennis is an example of _____.

c) In weightlifting, athletes direct their aggression against _____.

d) A runner's commitment to training, even in the cold and wet, shows an _____.

Goal setting

Setting goals can help you in all areas, not just sport. Below is a form for recording your goals and checking how well you met them.

My goals for: _____

Goal 1: _____

Goal 2: _____

How I did

Goal 1: 0   1   2   3   4   5   6   7   8   9   10
         Terrible   Good   Excellent

Goal 2: 0   1   2   3   4   5   6   7   8   9   10
         Terrible   Good   Excellent

Comment: _____

Try this out for different kinds of goals. For example:

a) your next piece of homework. Your goals could be about the time you spend and reducing the number of mistakes you make.

b) your next sports training session.

NAME

Arousal and relaxation

1 Choose one person from the class to be a speaker.

a) Allow the person to relax. Take his or her pulse for 15 seconds. Then send the person out of the room.

b) The class chooses a topic on which the speaker will make a speech. For example, it could be a sport or a favourite TV serial.

c) Tell the speaker the topic. Allow them a few minutes to prepare their thoughts. The speech should not last more than 4 minutes.

d) Take the speaker's pulse before the speech.

e) After the speech, take the speaker's pulse again.

f) What conclusions can you draw about the speaker's arousal level?

PULSE AT FIRST	PULSE BEFORE SPEECH	PULSE AFTER SPEECH	CONCLUSION

2 Choose someone who likes strong coffee but has not drunk any within the last 24 hours.

a) Take the person's pulse.

b) He or she now drinks a strong cup of coffee.

c) 20 minutes later, take the person's pulse again.

d) Has there been a change? Explain why.

PULSE BEFORE COFFEE	PULSE AFTER COFFEE	DIFFERENCE	REASON

3 You need two groups of 5 people (evenly matched in sporting ability) to do wall squats, and a person to act as timer.

a) Group A does wall squats in private. The timer records how long each person holds the squat.

b) Group B does the same thing in front of the class, who watch quietly without any comment.

c) Which group does better? _____

Can you explain why? _____

Arousal and relaxation

1 This graph shows the effect of arousal on performance.

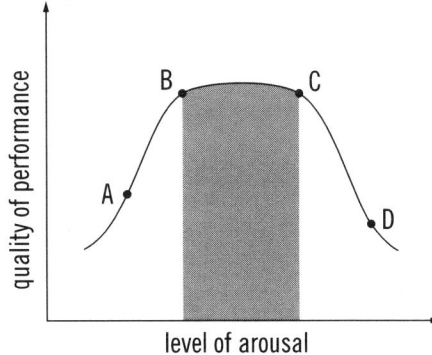

a) Where on the curve should you be, to give your best performance?
_____

b) At A, do you need to calm down or get more psyched up, in order to improve your performance?
_____

c) Name one way to bring about this change.
_____

d) Name one technique that would help you move from D to C on the curve.
_____

2 This graph shows the inverted U curves for three sports men, Mike, Ben and Joe.

The dots mark their position on the curves.

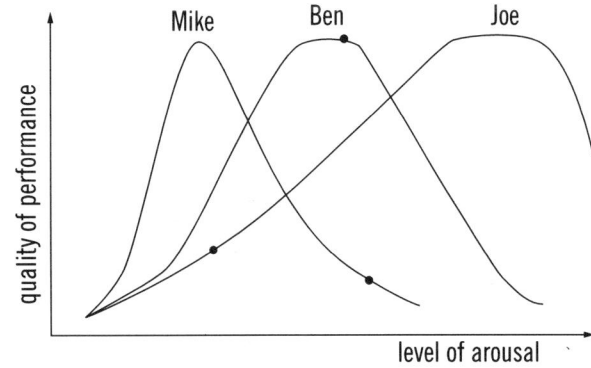

a) Who is giving the best performance?
_____

b) Who may be looking laid back or even bored?
_____

c) Who is probably trembling and sweating profusely?
_____

d) One is a snooker player, one a basketball player and one a weightlifter. Which is which? Explain your answer.
_____

Sports injuries

1 Name three different sports where the following bones may be broken:

	SPORT 1	SPORT 2	SPORT 3
the collar bone			
the bones in the arm			
the bones in the leg			

2 The knee joint (shown here) can often be damaged in many different sports.

a) Indicate on the diagram where damage could occur.

b) Make a note of the sport and circumstances in which these knee injuries occur.

c) What medical treatment might be carried out to treat or repair the damage?

_____

_____

_____

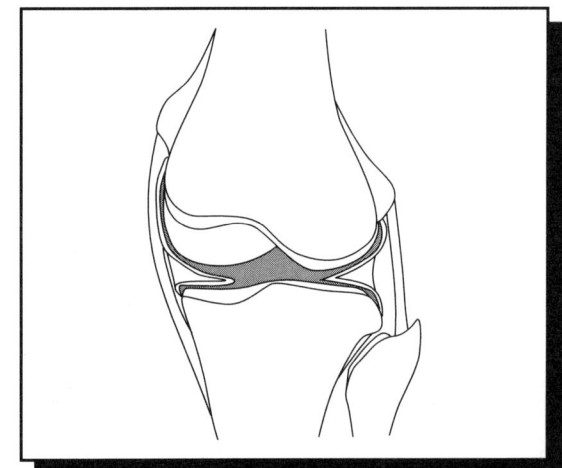

3 For each activity list the likely hazards, including hazards to onlookers.

SPORT	LIKELY HAZARD
Pole vaulting	
Throwing the javelin	

PE to 16   Worksheet 45   © Oxford University Press

Sports injuries

Here we show how to prevent injuries by doing a warm-up before the sports activity and a cool-down after it. You should spend 20–30 minutes on both activities. After the warm-up move on to the main activity as soon as you can.

1 Give three reasons for doing a warm-up and three reasons for doing a cool-down.

WARM-UP	COOL-DOWN
◆	◆
◆	◆
◆	◆

2 Complete the diagrams by writing in the boxes the benefits that can be gained by the parts of the body indicated, from each activity.

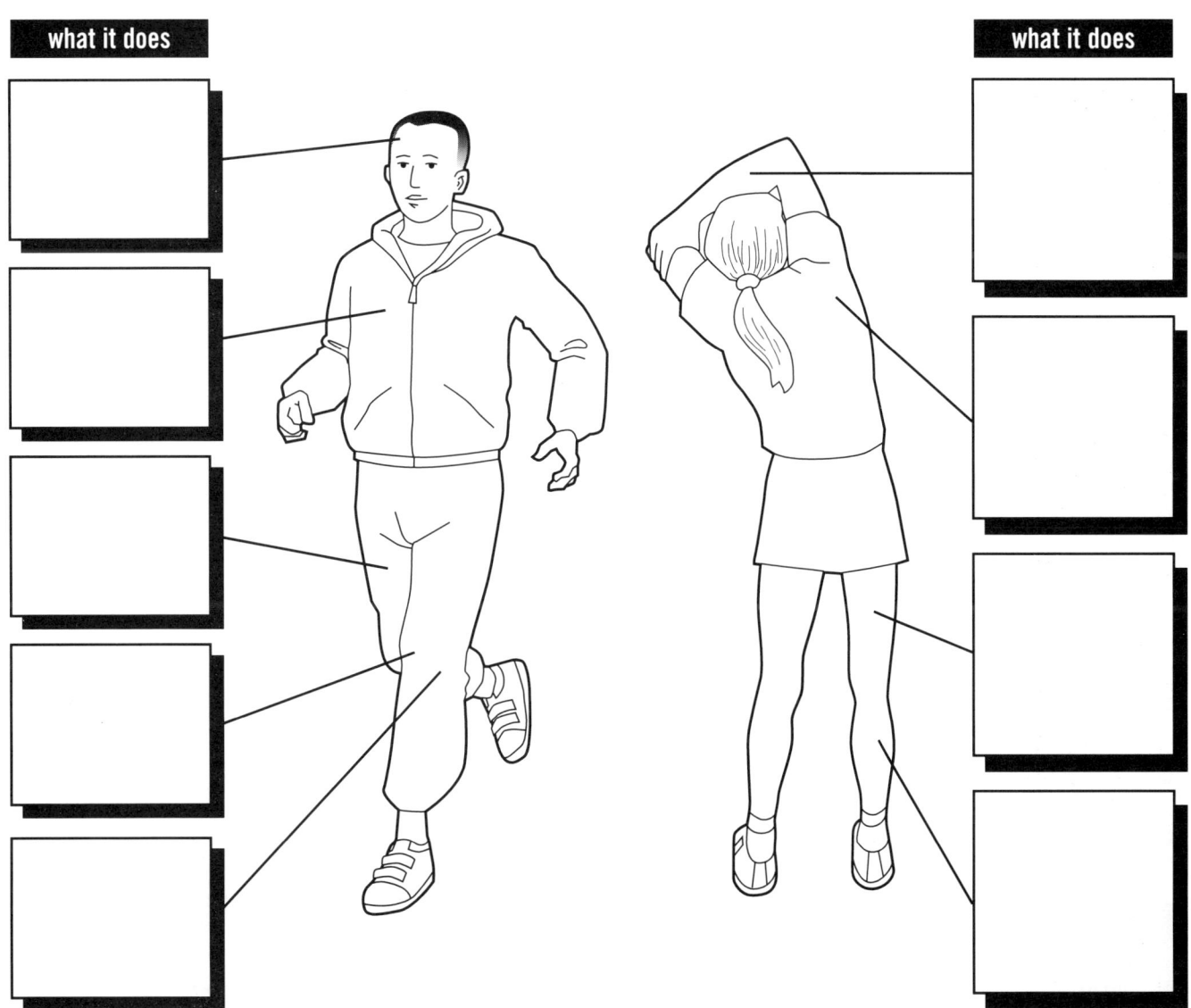

PE to 16 — Worksheet 46 — © Oxford University Press

What to do in an emergency

If someone is knocked out during a sporting activity, or has a fit, this is what to do.
Put the person into the recovery position – in the order as shown – and then get medical help.

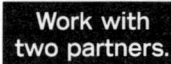
Work with two partners.

A One person acts as the casualty. A second reads the instructions. A third carries them out.

B Switch roles and repeat.

C Switch roles again. But this time the instructions are not read aloud. Instead the reader checks that the job is being done properly.

Step 1	With the casualty lying on his back, tilt the head back and chin up to open the airway.
Step 2	Straighten the legs.
Step 3	Move the arm nearest to you so that it looks like the arm of a police officer stopping traffic. 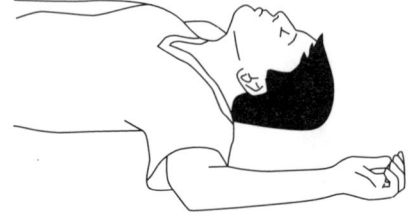
Step 4	Bring the other arm across the chest. Arrange so that the casualty's cheek rests on the back of this hand. Keep your hand on this hand for step 5. 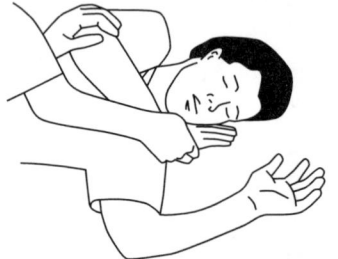
Step 5	With your other hand, reach across the casualty's far leg. Lift it so that the knee bends to a right angle. Then pull it to roll the casualty towards you. 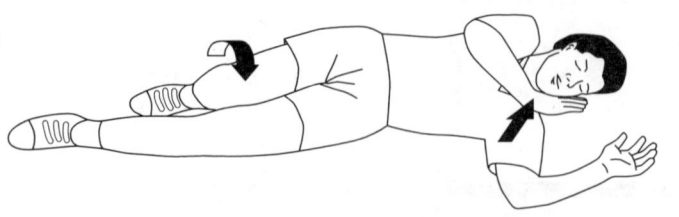
Step 6	Once the casualty is on his side, gently tilt the head back to keep the airway open. Use his hand under the cheek to hold it like that.

PE to 16 — Worksheet 47 — © Oxford University Press

NAME

What to do in an emergency

Imagine this scene

You are in the middle of a hockey match.

The centre-forward and centre-half collide at speed.

The centre-half is sitting crumpled on the ground, moaning that her knee hurts.

The centre forward is lying still with her eyes closed.

You are asked to help.

What should you do? [No, don't panic!]

Look at the centre-forward first as her injuries could be more serious.

1 Explain how you would deal with the situation using the DRABC principle:

   D is for Danger: _____

   R is for Response: _____

   A is for Airway: _____

   B is for Breathing: _____

   C is for Circulation: _____

2 Now complete the following:

   Dial _____ for emergency. _____

   _____

3 Having looked after the centre-forward it is now time to help the centre-half.
Follow the RICE principle. What does this mean she should do? Annotate the diagrams below.

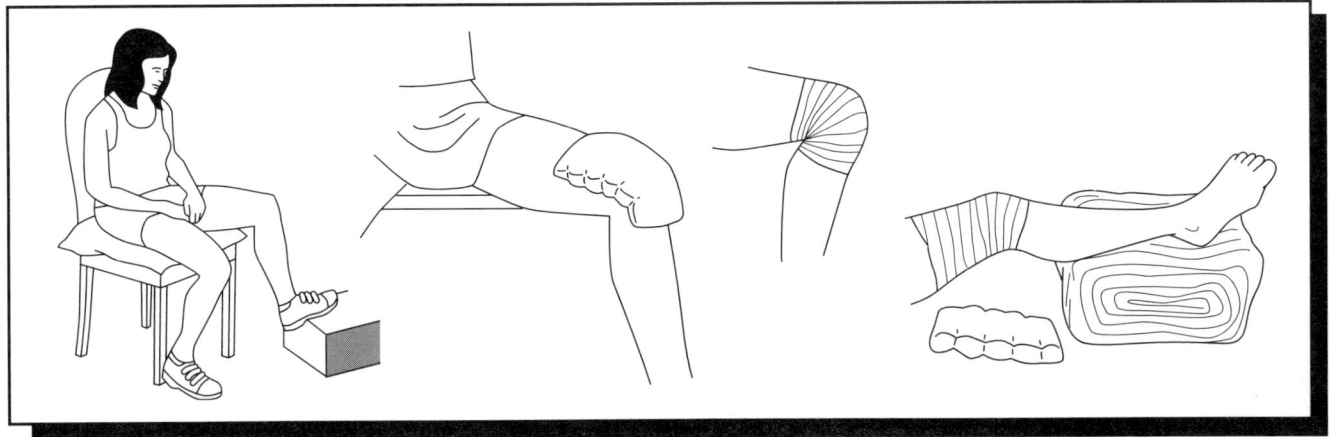

PE to 16   Worksheet 48   © Oxford University Press

Leisure, recreation or sport?

1 Is it a leisure activity (L), a sport (S), or recreation (R)? Explain why.

	L/S/R	WHY?
playing netball at lunchtime at school		
eating meals at home		
going to the cinema		
sleeping at night		
cycling to school		
playing cards with your friends		
rollerblading in the park		
a canoe trip in the summer holidays		
playing rugby union for your country		
netball practice after school		

2 The map shows part of a coastal town. It is not drawn to scale.

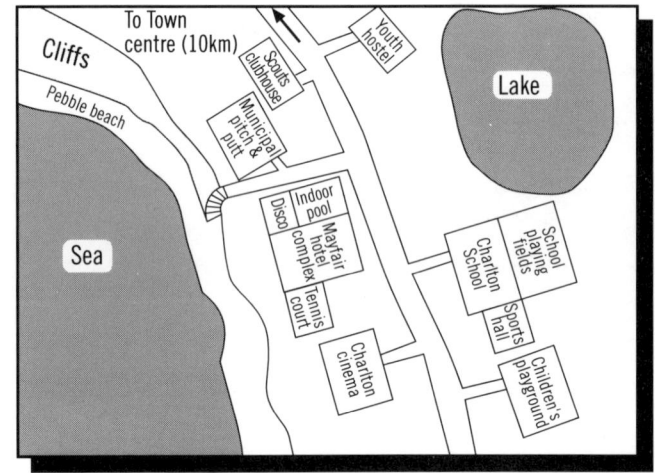

This question is about the facilities for physical recreation that appear on the map. Identify:

a) two natural facilities

b) two outdoor built facilities

c) two indoor built facilities

d) one facility provided by private enterprise

e) two provided by voluntary organizations

f) two provided by the local authority

Leisure, recreation or sport?

You will need:
- a map of the local area
- Yellow Pages or local Thomson directory
- Access to the internet if possible.

1 List the facilities for leisure, physical recreation and sports in your area, say within a radius of 5 km of your home. You will need the local map. (Yellow Pages, the local Thomson directory or the internet will help.)

2 Try to find out where the money comes from to fund each facility and mark whether it is a public sector, private sector or voluntary organization.

Local sports, recreation and leisure facilities

	PUBLIC SECTOR	PRIVATE SECTOR	VOLUNTARY

Sport for all?

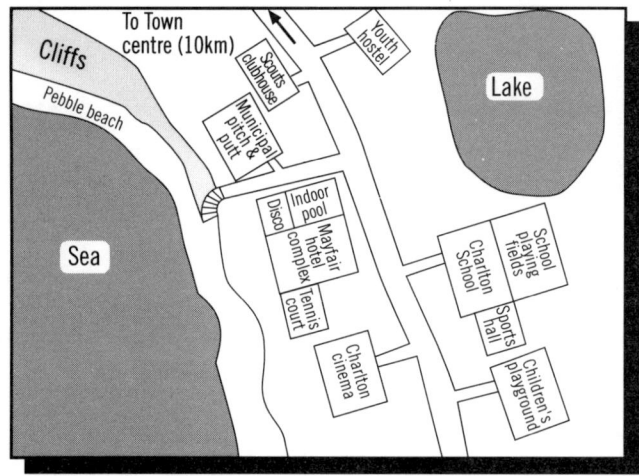

You have met this map before (on page 50). However, suppose you are a local authority planner. You want to develop the lake at the coastal town as a recreational facility.

1 Suggest some activities that could take place there.

_____
_____
_____

2 List all the different groups that might use the lake.

_____
_____
_____

3 Identify any conflicts that might arise between the activities.
What steps could you take to avoid them?

_____
_____
_____

4 If you can come up with a project that involves the local community and the school, you might obtain a Lottery Sports Fund grant. Suggest a suitable project.

_____

5 Will you need to build anything round the lake? What? Why?

_____
_____
_____

Sport for all?

Favourite physical activities

Walking	Running	Cricket
Swimming	Football	Darts
Keep fit/yoga	Badminton	Tenpin bowling/skittles
Cycling	Tennis	Fishing
Weight lifting/training	Squash	Bowls
Golf	Horse riding	Table tennis

The table below shows results from surveys carried out around the UK.

Thousands of people aged 16 and over were asked about their leisure activities.

The main physical activities are listed above.

a) Look at the table below. Which of the age groups is most active?

b) Had all groups become more active by 1998?

c) For which group did participation increase most, between 1990 and 1995?

d) Overall, do you think the aim of 'sport for all' has been achieved yet? Explain.

Percentage of age group taking part in at least one activity from the list above.

YEAR	16–19	20–24	25–29	30–44	45–59	60–69	70 AND OVER
1990	86	77	74	71	56	47	26
1995	86	80	77	73	64	51	33
1999	83	82	81	76	64	53	35

Sport in other countries

a) Start a tally chart with these headings:

Europe, North America, South America, Africa, Asia, Australasia.

b) Now list all the gold-medal winners from the 1996 Olympics. (Try the library.)

c) For each winner, put a mark in the correct place on your tally chart.

Which region won the most medals?

Which won least?

Can you explain why?

NAME

Women in sport

Debate topic

The main reason why women participate less in organized sport is because they have other priorities.

Divide the class into four, so that each of you takes the point of view of *one* of the four people shown here.

A female athlete who trains full time. She has a degree in sports administration and has ambitions to take up media presentation. She has strong views on why women should show what they can do. Receives funding and sponsorship. Would love to see more women at the top in sport.

A male psychologist who has written books on the differences between men and women – *Men Like Mars, Women Like Galaxy*. He is interested in the different motivations inspiring men and women.

17-year-old student, female, whose ambition is to become a top model and dancer. Likes to look 'a million dollars'. Although she is dating a famous sportsman she would never go on to a sports field if she could help it! A big disappointment to her mother who was a gold-medal-winning athlete and a model!

Sports-mad male, 22. Captain of rugby and athletics at university. He is an old-fashioned sexist who would simply prefer knocking around with the lads. However, he did enjoy playing in a mixed rugby game last season! His uncle is coach to a ladies football team; he has been seen at their matches shouting encouragement.

1 Write some notes on all the points you can think of to support the argument or point of view of the person you are role-playing. (**Remember** that you are acting the role of another person and need to see the issues as that person would see them.) You are going to be in a forum to discuss the statement at the top of this page.

2 Prepare some questions you would like to put to your opponents on the panel. Each group can make a panel and another group or groups provide the chairperson and audience. The chairperson is responsible for organizing the discussion and for making sure that it runs smoothly.

3 After the introduction by the chairperson, each member of the panel can make a short statement about their position and what they think about women's priorities in relation to sport.

4 The chairperson then asks for the first round of questions – one to each speaker – but each member of the panel should be allowed to comment if they wish. Then there can be questions from the audience – addressed to the whole panel or to individual speakers.

5 At the end of the session, discuss how you think the role-play went.

Women in sport

1. What sports do girls in your school or college play? Look at activities that are offered:

   a) in PE lessons _____
   _____

   b) for extra-curricular sport _____
   _____

   c) in your local area _____
   _____

   Present your findings in the form of a table.

2. Look at the sports programmes listed in television guides for one week (include satellite and digital).

   How many women's sports are mentioned?
   _____

   How much airtime is given to women's sports compared to men's?
   _____

3. Design a poster for a new or existing sports club at your school or college.

   You are trying to attract new members, particularly women.

PE to 16   Worksheet 54   © Oxford University Press

NAME

Sports organizations

Divide your group into two teams, with one person being 'quiz controller/scorer'. Each team should choose a representative to act as spokesperson when giving answers.

The quiz controller asks each team a question in turn. A team scores 2 points for a right answer. If they get it wrong, or don't know, the question is passed to the other team – for a possible bonus of 1. When all the questions below have been used, you could make up some more of your own to give to the quiz controller (you must know the answer though).

Quiz controller: 'All of these questions are about sports organizations.'

1. The FA is the governing body for football in England. Name the world governing body for association football.
2. Which organization has five interlocked rings as its logo?
3. What do the initials CCPR stand for?
4. Where are the headquarters of the Marylebone Cricket Club (MCC)?
5. How many sports councils are there in the UK?
6. What do the initials LTA stand for?
7. Name two governing bodies of sport.
8. What do the initials ASA stand for?
9. True or false? The International Olympic Committee leads the fight against drug abuse in sport.
10. How often are the Olympics held?
11. What do the initials SAF stand for?
12. Which sports agency's motto is 'Giving Britons a Sporting Chance'?
13. What is the name for the organization governing yoga in Britain?
14. Which organization is responsible for PE in the UK?

Answers

1 FIFA 2 The Olympic movement 3 Central Council for Physical Recreation 4 Lord's 5 five 6 Lawn Tennis Association 8 Amateur Swimming Association 9 true 10 4 years 11 Sports Aid Foundation 12 SAF 13 The British Wheel of Yoga 14 Department of Education and Employment

Sports organizations

1 Sport England can provide data for most sports and leisure activities. Find out about your nearest regional sports office. Which member of your regional Sport England office is in charge of your favourite sport for the area where you live?

2 The English Table Tennis Association has:

- 40 county associations
- 50,000 players
- 4500 clubs
- 11,000 teams
- 270 local leagues

Find out about the structure, number of organizations and players for a sport you like.

3 The Central Council for Physical Recreation (CCPR) is split into six divisions:

Find the names of six local clubs or organizations which are represented by the six divisions of the CCPR.

Games and sports (17 affiliated members)	1.
Movement and dance (27)	2.
Water recreation (26)	3.
Major spectator sports (130)	4.
Outdoor pursuits (48)	5.
Interested organizations (102)	6.

4 The CCPR Junior Sports Leaders Award (JSA) is aimed at students in the final two years of their PE in school (ie at Key Stage 4). Find as much information as possible about the JSA.

Do you think that this is a useful qualification to have? _____

5 Sport England has created standard plans for sports centres: Standard Approach to Sports Halls (SASH). Local authorities all over the country can use these plans to build sports centres that look very similar.

a) In what ways is this a good idea? Think of as many as you can.

b) Can you think of any way in which it's a bad idea?

Funding sport

Work in a group.

1 Is your school or club in need of some new sports equipment, or repairs to sports facilities?

Draw up a list of what needs doing.

Choose one item for which to raise money. (Don't be too ambitious. Choose something realistic.)

2 Describe what is needed and find out roughly what it would cost. You may need help from your teacher for this.

3 Now have a brainstorming session about how to raise the money. In brainstorming (example below), everyone calls out an idea in turn, without worrying about whether it is stupid. One person writes the ideas on a board or flipchart as they are called out. Allow say 12 minutes for this activity.

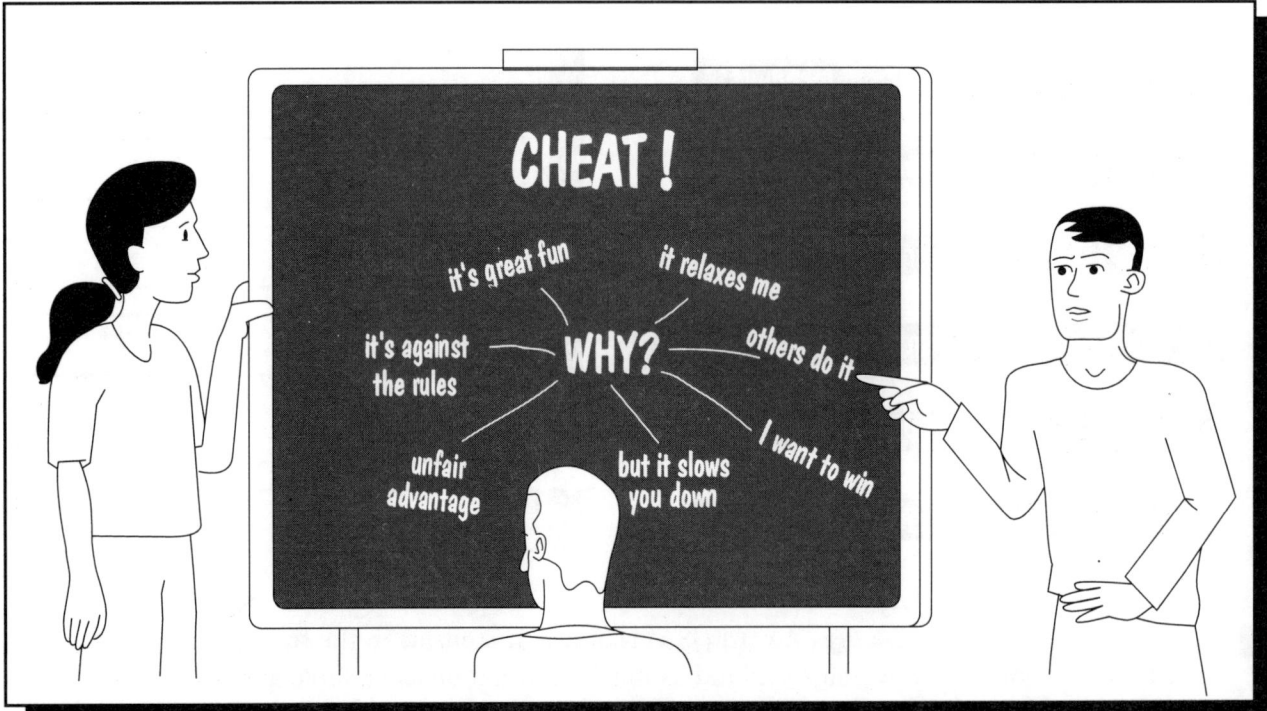

4 Now go through the list and pick out four or five good ideas. Decide how much money you could raise from each one.

5 Write a project proposal from your group to your head teacher or club chairperson, explaining what you want to do and why, and setting out your plans very clearly. Request permission to go ahead with the project.

Funding sport

Sponsorship is where a business provides support for an event, team or individual.

The business gets publicity in exchange. Its name or logo is displayed on kit, hoardings and programmes.

Complete the following. Add some of your own examples.

INDIVIDUAL/TEAM/EVENT	SPONSOR'S NAME	SPORT IT IS CONNECTED TO
Naseem Hamed		
	Sharp	Soccer
London Marathon		
Tiger Woods		
First Class Sunday League		Cricket
	Ora	Soccer
	Nike	Basketball
Yorkshire CCC		
	JJB Sports	Rugby league
England		Rugby union
	Cellnet	Soccer
World Championships		Snooker
FA Cup		
McLaren		
	Beefeater Gin	Rowing
Grand National		Horse racing
Eastbourne Championships		

Worksheet 58

Sport around the world

1 Copy and complete this table about past Olympics.

DATE	HOST CITY	ISSUE
1936	Berlin	Games used as Nazi propaganda
	Melbourne	
	Mexico City	
1976		
1980		
	Los Angeles	
1988		
	Barcelona	
1996		
	Sydney	

2 These are some of the jobs carried out in Sydney to prepare for the 2000 Olympics:

- new sports venues built and others updated
- ageing bridges, streets and sewers overhauled
- the airport renovated
- detailed plans made for safety and security
- several billion Australian dollars raised to cover the costs
- over 12 million tickets distributed around the world.

a) List all the different kinds of people needed for these jobs. Include architects and engineers, for example.

b) How will the Games benefit Sydney's citizens? Think of as many ways as you can.

c) Do you think the Olympic Games are a success? Explain your answer.

3 The Atlanta Games in 1996 made only a very small profit. The Sydney Games in 2000 are expected to do the same. One reason is the high cost of security. Another is that the world expects a more dazzling display each time.

a) Give reasons why security is a big concern.

b) Do you think display and pageantry are necessary for the games? Explain your answer.

c) In spite of small profits, countries are lining up to host the games. Why should they want to do this?

Sport around the world

You will need:
- a calculator
- an atlas or encyclopedia
- some spare paper.

Look at the top 26 countries in the final medal table for the Atlanta Olympics below. How many of these would you describe as 'developing countries'?

1996 Atlanta Olympics – medal table

COUNTRY/MEDALS		POPULATION	MEDALS ÷ POP.	COUNTRY/MEDALS		POPULATION	MEDALS ÷ POP.
USA	101			Netherlands	19		
Germany	65			Poland	17		
Russia	63			Spain	17		
China	50			Bulgaria	15		
Australia	40			Britain	15		
France	37			Belarus	15		
Italy	35			Brazil	15		
South Korea	27			Japan	14		
Cuba	25			Czech Republic	11		
Ukraine	23			Kazakhstan	11		
Canada	22			Greece	8		
Hungary	21			Kenya	8		
Romania	20			Sweden	8		

1 Draw up a table of the top developing nations from the medal-winning results.

2 Using an atlas or encyclopedia, find out the population for each of these 26 countries. You would expect that countries with bigger populations would do better since they have more people to choose from. Is this so?

3 Using your calculator and your data for the top 26 countries, divide the total number of medals by the population in millions. For example, for Britain the figures would be $15 \div 65 = 0.27$.

4 Redraw the table for the top 26 countries, placing the country with the highest number of medals per head of population at the top. Is there a difference between the two tables?

Sport and the media

NAME

Work in a group.

The media are all the means by which information is delivered: books, newspapers, magazines, radio, TV, films, video and the internet.

Here are some **positive** and **negative** ways in which the media can affect sport.

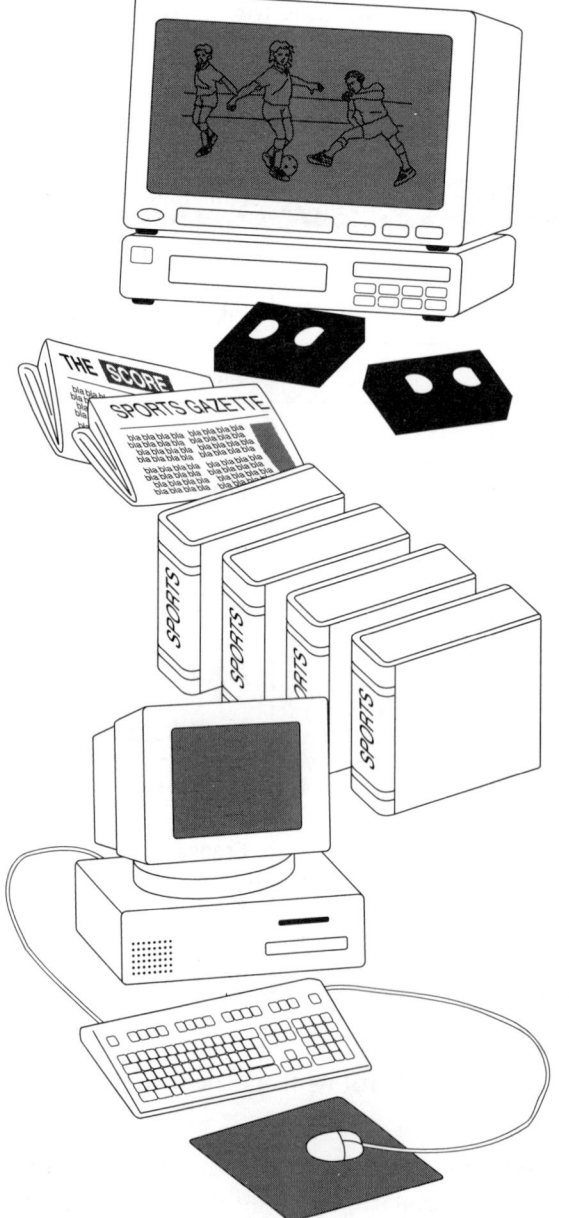

POSITIVE

- Media coverage promotes sport. People learn about a sport and may want to try it out.

- The media helps to educate and inform sports fans, which is healthy for sport.

- Television programmes, videos and books can help you learn and improve your sports skills.

- The media creates sports stars who inspire young people and act as role models for them.

- A sport with lots of media coverage (especially television) finds it easier to get sponsorship.

NEGATIVE

- The media puts extra pressure on managers and coaches to get results. They may be hounded out of their jobs if they fail.

- Sports stars lose privacy. Their private lives get reported on.

- A sport may get too much exposure. Some people think this is happening to football.

- The media may sensationalise sports news and events to attract more viewers or readers.

- Sports that get little or no media attention find it very difficult to get sponsorship.

1 You have been asked to appear on a programme to talk about the impact of the media on sport today. Decide what viewpoint you wish to present. Make some notes to support your argument.

2 As a group, hold the interview in a 'mock studio' with one person asking the questions and the others being interviewed. You could video or tape record the session.

Sport and the media

You will need:
A tabloid and a broadsheet newspaper for the same day.

1 Study the sports pages of both papers, then fill in the table.

UK press sports coverage

		TABLOID	BROADSHEET
Title			
Number of sports covered			
Number of 'male-oriented' pieces			
Number of 'female-oriented' pieces			
Percentage of sports pages devoted to:	Photographs		
	Headlines		
	Text		
	Adverts		

2 Pick the main sports event of the day. Compare coverage in the tabloid and the broadsheet newspapers you have.

a) What differences do you notice?

b) Do you agree with these statements?

The tabloids tend to:

- go for sensational headlines
- take a strong line of approval or disapproval
- pay little attention to minority sports.

The quality press tend to:

- go for in-depth coverage and comment
- do more thoughtful analysis
- give more coverage to minority sports.

Other issues in sport

1 **True or false?** Explain your answer.

a) If you are an amateur athlete it means you are not as good as the professionals.   T ☐ F ☐

_____

b) Amateur athletes in athletics can't accept prize money.   T ☐ F ☐

_____

c) Appearance money is what you get for wearing your sponsor's logo.   T ☐ F ☐

_____

d) Both amateur and professional golfers can compete in an open golf tournament.   T ☐ F ☐

_____

e) Open sports never offer prize money.   T ☐ F ☐

_____

f) If no-one wanted to watch sport there would be no professionals.   T ☐ F ☐

_____

2 a) From the boxed list choose the two sports where you think:

- violence between participants is most likely   _____ _____
- violence between participants is least likely   _____ _____
- violence among supporters is most likely   _____ _____
- violence among supporters is least likely   _____ _____

> tennis
> gymnastics
> swimming
> rugby
> volleyball
> football

b) Do you think there is a connection between violence among spectators and the nature of the sport?

c) How could you test this theory?

d) Design a project for this purpose. Describe it as fully as you can.

3 **'Football causes violence.'**

Do you agree? Explain why.

_____

_____

_____

> You are the managing director of a football club. Describe what steps you could take to:
> - combat racism
> - combat hooliganism
> - attract families to watch live sport.

Other issues in sport

The division between amateurs and professionals had its origins in the class system.

Amateurs were gentlemen who could afford to play a sport, often full time, for pleasure.

Professionals were lower-class people who earned money from sport, often by doing something for a wager (bet) or by competing for prizes against others.

For example, gentlemen with coaches and horses had footmen. If you were the gambling type you might choose an athletic footman, and pay him something to compete in walking races against your friends' footmen. You'd put a bet on the race.

Cricket was popular among gentlemen. In the 18th century gentlemen's cricket clubs employed some lower-class cricketers who were called **players**. They were paid to look after the grounds, coach the gentlemen and play against them in matches.

As sports became more organized, tension between the amateur gentlemen and working-class professionals grew. In 1866 the Amateur Athletics Club was set up by gentlemen. Working-class men were excluded because it was felt manual labour gave them an advantage in strength.

In 1880 the club became the Amateur Athletics Association. It redefined an amateur as someone who gained no financial reward from a sport. The working classes were allowed in.

1 Find out more about the early professional cricketers. Write a short essay about them.

2 Look at this old poster for a match between gentlemen and players.

What do you notice about the way their names are listed?

_____
_____
_____
_____

Gentlemen versus Players Cricket Match

Saturday June 11th, 2pm, Croxley Green

Gentlemen
Sir Algernon Knox-Leonard (c.)
Mr. W. Grace
Lt. A. N. Alternate
Prof. G. Hales
Mr. F. Truperson

Players
G. Oliver (c.)
W. Grayson
A. Mallarkey
R. Willis

A famous example of someone walking for a wager was Captain Barclay. In 1800 he walked 1000 miles in 1000 hours for 1000 guineas.

Try to find out about Captain Barclay.

Who put up the money?

Where did he walk?

Wordsearch

Answer the clues below and write the word in the spaces.
The shaded boxes spell out the name of a banned substance (8, 7).

1 A connective tissue connecting two bones together.
2 The building component of our diet.
3 Breathing out.
4 Sport played indoors with a shuttlecock.
5 Hormone produced in females.
6 Skills that are not affected by surrounding factors.
7 Substance that produces pain in muscles.
8 The body's first choice for energy.
9 Establishing objectives to work towards.
10 Help to develop ability to change pace.
11 Treatment which involves doing exercises.
12 Helps prepare the body for physical exercise.
13 Water sport or recreation in a narrow boat.
14 Torvill and Dean are associated with this sport.
15 You need to drink to prevent this.

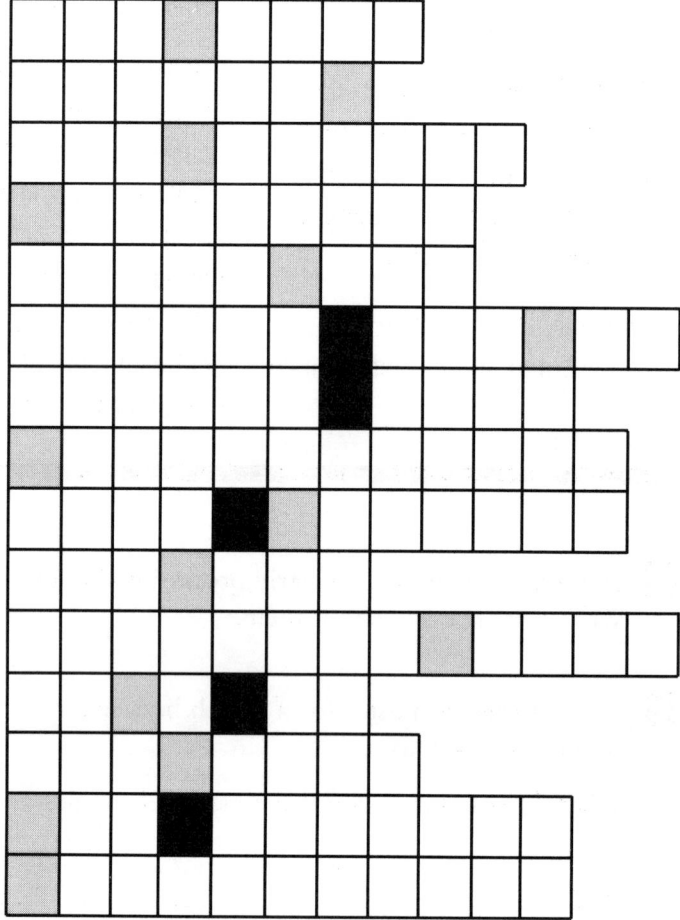

Worksheet 65

Wordsearch

Find as many words to do with sport and recreation as you can in the grid.
Don't forget to check up, down, across, diagonally and backwards.

C	A	R	D	I	O	V	A	S	C	U	L	A	R	M
O	T	X	O	K	S	E	L	C	S	U	M	J	E	S
O	H	I	O	S	U	P	E	R	S	T	A	R	S	I
R	L	G	F	E	D	S	U	F	E	V	I	E	P	C
D	E	V	E	L	O	P	M	E	N	T	J	C	I	A
I	T	Q	B	O	X	O	G	M	T	E	A	I	R	R
N	I	A	R	P	S	R	F	A	I	R	W	R	A	S
A	C	T	I	V	I	T	Y	L	F	L	O	G	T	T
T	S	P	E	E	D	F	Z	E	Y	N	U	R	O	S
I	X	Y	E	K	C	O	H	L	O	D	A	J	R	E
O	N	P	W	C	Q	R	R	T	P	I	S	W	Y	T
N	E	Z	A	R	H	A	E	G	N	I	N	K	S	S
J	T	M	R	I	E	L	A	M	P	I	N	S	Y	T
M	B	E	O	C	E	L	T	J	O	I	N	T	S	C
E	A	M	U	K	W	I	N	Z	S	S	E	R	T	S
D	L	O	S	E	K	K	S	P	O	R	T	E	E	M
I	L	R	A	T	P	S	Y	B	G	U	R	J	M	I
A	T	Y	L	L	I	M	P	Y	T	I	L	I	G	A

Worksheet 66

> **Note for teachers**
>
> The following questions can be used as a mock examination using the sample cover sheet provided. Alternatively thay can be used separately as required.

General Certificate of Secondary Education

PHYSICAL EDUCATION

Mock Examination

Total time allowed: 2 hours

Important notes

Answer **all** the questions.

Write your answers clearly. You can make notes but cross them out clearly.

Use diagrams wherever they will help your answer.

The total number of marks available is 100 and there are 5 extra marks available for good spelling, grammar and punctuation.

The number of marks available for each part of each question is shown in brackets.

Section A

Health related exercise

1 *Total for this question: 15 marks*

    (a) Describe fully where the following bones are found in the body.
        (i)   radius *(2 marks)*
        (ii) clavicle *(2 marks)*
        (iii) patella *(2 marks)*

    (b) Give one example of where each of the following joints is found on the body. In each case state which bones form the joint.
        (i)   hinge *(2 marks)*
        (ii) ball and socket *(2 marks)*

    (c) Explain and describe how physical movement takes place through the combined action of muscles and bones. *(5 marks)*

2 *Total for this question: 15 marks*

    (a) What is meant by the term R.I.C.E. when treating an injury which occurs during a games session. *(4 marks)*

    (b) A suitable warm-up and cool-down are important before and after taking part in a games activity. Describe the following:
        (i) two reasons why a warm-up is necessary *(2 marks)*
        (ii) two reasons why a cool-down is necessary *(2 marks)*

    (c) In three named physical activities, state one different safety consideration. Explain why. *(7 marks)*

3 *Total for this question: 15 marks*

    (a) Name three different body types, or somatotypes. *(3 marks)*

    (b) Describe ways in which drinking too much alcohol could have a bad effect on a performance. *(3 marks)*

    (c) Explain what is meant by the terms aerobic respiration and anaerobic respiration in relation to exercise. Give an example for each from a named physical/game activity. *(3 marks)*

    (d) Psychological factors can affect a performance. Name two such factors, and describe the effects they can have. *(6 marks)*

4   Total for this question: 15 marks

(a) Name three different types of strength. *(3 marks)*

(b) Define what is meant by being in a good state of health. *(3 marks)*

(c) Describe what is meant by fatigue and explain the effect it can have on a performance in a named game. *(3 marks)*

(d) Describe fully three personal hygiene rules a sports performer should follow. Explain why these hygiene rules should be encouraged. *(6 marks)*

Section B

Sport and society

5   **Total for this question: 20 marks**

(a) Facilities are vitally important for the provision of sport. State the importance of the following in deciding their location.

    (i) population *(2 marks)*

    (ii) access *(2 marks)*

    (iii) cost *(2 marks)*

    (iv) natural features *(2 marks)*

(b) There are many different groups of people who like to use sports facilities. Identify two types of user of sports facilities. Describe the specific types of provision and activities that should be provided for each user. *(6 marks)*

(c) Describe the effects that media coverage may be having on attendance at sporting events. Give examples from actual events to explain your answer fully. *(6 marks)*

6   Total for this question: 20 marks

(a) The number of people who take part in sport is increasing. How can the following help to influence participation in sport?

    (i) The way Physical Education is taught in schools. *(2 marks)*

    (ii) The facilities available in schools. *(2 marks)*

    (iii) Attitudes of parents *(2 marks)*

    (iv) Attitudes of peers/friends *(2 marks)*

(b) Explain the reasons why there may now be more available leisure time. Describe the ways that the leisure industry provides for this. *(6 marks)*

(c) State the governing body of a named game/activity and describe its roles and responsibilities. *(6 marks)*